Philanthropists
and Their Legacies

PROFILES

Philanthropists
and Their Legacies

T 19339

Carol G. Traub

The Oliver Press, Inc.
Minneapolis

*For my loving family and devoted friends whose support
and great expectations spurred me on, with special thanks
to K.R.T. for invaluable aid and comfort.*

The Oliver Press, Inc.
Charlotte Square
5707 West 36th Street
Minneapolis, MN 55416-2510

Library of Congress Cataloging-in-Publication Data

Traub, Carol G.
Philanthropists and their legacies / Carol G. Traub.
p.   cm. — (Profiles)
Includes bibliographical references and index.
Summary: Describes how people like Alfred Nobel, Cecil Rhodes,
Andrew Carnegie, Julius Rosenwald, and John D. and Catherine T.
MacArthur first made and then gave away vast sums of money.
ISBN 1-881508-42-0 (library binding)
1. Philanthropists—Biography—Juvenile literature. [1. Philanthropists.]
I. Title. II. Series: Profiles (Minneapolis, Minn.)
HV27.T73   1997
361.7'4'092273—dc21
[B]   96-6520
                                                            CIP
                                                            AC

ISBN: 1-881508-42-0
Profiles XXII
Printed in the United States of America

03 02 01 00 99 98 97   8 7 6 5 4 3 2 1

Contents

The Nobel Prize has become a prestigious legacy of inventor Alfred Nobel. Here geneticist Har Gobind Khorana receives his 1968 prize in physiology and medicine from King Gustaf Adolf of Sweden.

Foreword

*T*his book, while giving the brief story behind nine prominent philanthropists, does so much more for the reader. By retelling the lives of these people, it demonstrates that an individual's desire to help others is the most important factor in a donation. While these stories profile those who amassed gigantic fortunes, every person has the potential to do something positive for others and thus become a philanthropist.

I never thought of myself as a philanthropist. As cofounder of H & R Block, Inc., I was a successful tax preparer with a wonderful family. I had advised numerous clients to make charitable contributions because of the substantial possible tax advantages. In addition to the financial benefits, I saw the pleasure they received from making these gifts.

In 1978, I was diagnosed with terminal lung cancer and given 90 days to live. Another doctor said he would cure me so that I could work for other victims of this disease. In the ensuing 18 years, my wife and I have devoted our lives to helping others who have been stricken with cancer by starting several programs to help cancer patients. All services are provided free of charge, and none of the programs engage in fund raising. We do not look on these activities as charity, but as repaying a tremendous debt we owe. The letters we receive make our work far more rewarding than trying to earn more money.

It is important for people to realize that once they have the comfort of their family assured, it is then time to do something for the community. *Philanthropists and Their Legacies* demonstrates that the direction of the philanthropy is far less important than the act of trying to help. I truly believe this book will inspire many of its readers not only to succeed, but also to become philanthropists themselves.

—Richard R. Bloch
Honorary Chairman
H & R Block, Inc.

Introduction

*T*he word *philanthropy* comes from two Greek words: *philo*, meaning love, and *anthropos*, meaning human beings. When put together, philanthropy means goodwill to fellow humans, with an active effort to promote their welfare. Thus, a *philanthropist* is a person who makes an effort to improve the well-being of others through charitable acts or donations.

This book profiles nine individuals whose legacies have given clear meaning to the definition of philanthropy. These dynamic people amassed vast wealth during their lifetimes—and then gave away most of their riches for the benefit of others.

Each of them came from a different background and possessed individual interests and talents. Yet they all shared some similar attributes. They earned their wealth through their own determination and ingenuity. They were also risk-takers who worked toward their goals with a sense of purpose and strength of character. And all of them looked into a window of opportunity and directed their energies toward a vision of success.

Many events enabled these great philanthropists to reach positions of wealth and influence. One important factor was the introduction of power-driven machinery in

The Industrial Revolution brought many changes, not all of them good. Children often worked long hours in factories instead of attending school. Philanthropist Andrew Carnegie began his career as a bobbin boy, working on machines similar to those pictured here.

England in the late 1700s, which increased dramatically the output of goods—and, consequently, of profits—compared to manufacturing by hand. The revolution in industry would bring about major changes in the economy of the Western world.

With the Industrial Revolution came the invention of new tools, new sources of power, and new ways of organizing production. The invention of dynamite; the discoveries of huge quantities of natural resources such as diamonds, gold, and oil; the development of steel; and improvements in mass merchandising gave impetus to economic growth. Many individuals profiled in this book took advantage of the unprecedented opportunities to achieve wealth offered by the Industrial Revolution.

As the world moved into the twentieth century, the many changes brought about by the Industrial Revolution had an extraordinary effect on people's lives. Inventions such as the telephone, electric lights, the automobile, and the airplane brought new comforts and convenience.

The early 1900s, however, were not a time of equal opportunity for sharing this wealth. Few women worked outside the home, and those who did usually held low-paying jobs. Women did not have the right to vote or to own property. Instead of attending school, many children worked in factories, where newly-arrived immigrants labored long hours in poor and often dangerous surroundings. African Americans, freed from slavery after the Civil War, still faced poverty and prejudice.

In the early twentieth century, governments also took a less active role in trying to help people survive. Until the Sixteenth Amendment was ratified in 1913, the United States had no federal income tax. Consequently, there were not many federal programs for dealing with social problems, and people with little or no money had few places to turn to for aid. At the same time, business owners, with hardly any tax obligations, could accumulate fortunes more easily. Although numerous ambitious men gained considerable wealth under these favorable conditions, not all of them were generous, and many squandered or spent their money for selfish purposes.

The individuals profiled in this book, however, were motivated to make money as a measure of their success, not to spend on themselves. They wanted to give something back to the society that had offered them the opportunity to succeed. These philanthropists focused their giving toward relieving hardships, supporting education and the arts, addressing social ills, and promoting peace in the world.

The nine philanthropists in this book developed their attitudes toward giving from many different sources. Andrew Carnegie, Will Keith Kellogg, and George Eastman never forgot the hardships they had faced in their youth. John D. Rockefeller and Julius Rosenwald followed the traditions of charitable giving taught by their religions. Alfred Nobel and Cecil Rhodes hoped to find a place in history. John D. MacArthur and his wife,

Catherine, lived later in the century, when giving away wealth brought personal economic benefits because of higher income taxes.

Today, philanthropy is big business. Many millions of dollars are disbursed annually through charitable trusts or foundations. A *foundation*, defined as a legal and social instrument for applying private wealth to public purposes, is a nonprofit, nongovernmental organization. Foundations usually support research projects or public service endeavors in fields such as education, science, medicine, public health, or social welfare. Large foundations often hire many employees to carry out the decisions made by their trustees and directors. Some universities now offer courses of study in foundation management as a career option.

Walter H. Annenberg, the founder of *TV Guide* and other magazines, has given away nearly $1 billion. He has stated that "services to or in behalf of others must be in keeping with one's own good fortune in life." The creative and unselfish generosity of the philanthropists profiled in these pages exemplify that belief. Their legacies may inspire others to do the same.

Concerned about the destructive ways his inventions were used, Alfred Nobel (1833-1896) left his money to people who worked for peace and human progress.

14

1

Alfred Bernhard Nobel
Dynamite and Prizes

*E*very year on December 10, the anniversary of the death of inventor Alfred Nobel, the winners of the Nobel Prize receive their awards. This famous and prestigious prize recognizes accomplishments in science, literature, and economics as well as achievements toward world peace.

At ceremonies in Stockholm, Sweden and Oslo, Norway, each winner receives a gold medal, a diploma, and a substantial sum of money. In 1996, each prize was worth more than $1 million. Being named a Nobel laureate also earns these individuals the respect and honor of people throughout the world.

Alfred Nobel, the Swedish inventor who gave the world its most prestigious prizes, wanted to be remembered as a man of peace. A complex man, Nobel was reserved, often melancholy and brooding, but always absorbed in his work. Nobel's great wealth came from his many inventions. In his lifetime, he was granted more than 350 patents and owned 80 companies in 20 countries. One of his inventions—dynamite—literally changed the face of the earth, giving engineers the means to clear harbors and to construct railroads through mountains.

Other Nobel inventions, however, would take war and terrorism to levels of horror previously unknown. Near the end of his life, Nobel hoped that by rewarding "those who shall have conferred the greatest benefit on mankind," his legacy ultimately would be world peace and an end to suffering and destruction.

Alfred Bernhard Nobel was born near Stockholm, Sweden, on October 21, 1833. A sickly child, Alfred spent much of his early childhood in bed, entertained and tutored by his mother, Carolina Ahlsell Nobel. Alfred was eight before his health improved enough to allow him to join his two older brothers in public school. But because he was intelligent and quick to learn, he soon caught up in his studies.

Alfred's father, Immanuel, a self-taught and somewhat eccentric inventor, always expected his next project to make the family rich. Instead, due to a run of bad luck, he went bankrupt the year Alfred was born. Needing work, Immanuel left his family in Sweden and went to Russia, where the government offered him a contract to develop weapons such as mines and torpedoes.

By the time Alfred was nine, Immanuel's finances had improved, so he sent for his struggling family to join him in St. Petersburg. There Alfred and his brothers continued their education with private tutors.

Alfred possessed a capacity for learning well beyond his years. He read avidly, wrote poetry, and became fluent in Swedish, Russian, German, English, and French. By watching his father at work in his laboratory and asking questions, Alfred began to show promise as an inventor. When Alfred was 17, his father sent him abroad for two years. He traveled to the United States, Italy, and Germany, but he spent much of his time studying chemistry at a small laboratory in Paris, France. There he received the training he needed to work with his father and two brothers.

While Alfred was away, Immanuel and his two older sons were creating armaments for the Russian military. The weapons they devised used gunpowder, the only explosive known at that time. After Alfred's return to Russia, a chemistry professor demonstrated to the Nobel family the explosive qualities of a heavy, oily liquid he thought the Nobels might be able to use in their work. It was called nitroglycerin. There was a problem with the substance, however. Since its discovery by Ascanio Sobrero in 1847, it had never been put to use because no one had found a way to control it. As the Nobels watched, the visiting professor demonstrated its explosive properties. Immediately, Alfred recognized that nitroglycerin would be a great improvement over gunpowder.

The family business failed after the 1856 Treaty of Paris ended the Crimean War—and the Russian government's orders for weapons. So, in 1859, Alfred's parents returned to Sweden with their youngest son, Emil, while Alfred remained in Russia with his two older brothers. In Heleneborg, Sweden, near Stockholm, his father set up a laboratory to experiment with nitroglycerin. The problems of controlling this potentially powerful explosive seemed overwhelming because the substance was unpredictable in its reactions, as well as being difficult to store and transport safely.

Spurred on by the challenge, Alfred Nobel returned to Sweden in 1862 to help his father. He performed more than 50 experiments until he found a way to stabilize nitroglycerin. Discovering that nitroglycerin was set off by physical shock or intense heat, he devised a blasting cap that used gunpowder to ignite the nitroglycerin.

In his earlier experiments, Nobel had mixed the gunpowder together with the nitroglycerin. Now he kept the two explosives separated until the ignition. When he ignited a small measure of gunpowder in one

Alfred Nobel's initial ignition principle is illustrated in this drawing. A slow-burning fuse (A), inside of a cork or plug (B) and encased by fireproof packing (C), leads to the cap filled with gun powder (D). The fuse sets off the gunpowder, which in turn explodes the nitroglycerin (E). The long fuse gave operators time to clear the area before detonation. In 1864, Nobel patented his igniter, a crucial element in his invention of dynamite.

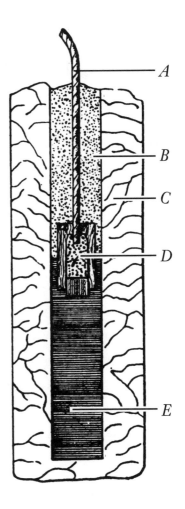

compartment of the cap, its small explosion detonated the nitroglycerin in the other compartment, which created a large explosion. His invention, which he called "Nobel's Patent Detonator," proved to be a safe and predictable way to ignite the nitroglycerin. In 1863, Nobel applied for a patent to protect his blasting cap invention.

Scientists hailed Nobel's invention as the most important development in the field of explosives since gunpowder had been invented in China in the eleventh century. Civil engineers immediately used nitroglycerin (labeled as blasting oil) to open seaports, cut through mountains, and excavate valuable minerals from underground mines.

Even though Nobel's blasting caps made nitroglycerin relatively safe to use, the nitroglycerin alone could still explode if it were not handled properly. Because of carelessness and a lack of understanding, many serious accidents began to occur. Although Nobel's company packed the substance with care and put warning labels on the cartons, workers remained ignorant about the potential for explosion from any kind of shock. When the cans holding the nitroglycerin leaked, workers would use the oily substance to lubricate their wagon axles or to oil their boots, causing injuries to themselves and others standing nearby.

In spite of these accidents, which the press called intolerable, industrial companies throughout the world still ordered Nobel's blasting product. But, bowing to public opinion, more and more governments began to ban nitroglycerin in their countries.

Determined to find a way to make the unpredictable substance safer to handle, Alfred, with the help of his father and younger brother, continued the experiments. Then on September 3, 1864, tragedy struck the Nobel family. The youngest Nobel son, twenty-year-old Emil, was working in the laboratory before leaving for college.

Suddenly, a violent explosion set off a ball of fire that burned the building to the ground. Emil and four other workers were killed instantly. Overcome with grief, Alfred's father, Immanuel, suffered a paralyzing stroke. He died eight years later on the anniversary of Emil's death.

In spite of his anguish over his brother's death, Alfred vowed to work even harder to solve the problems that had caused the explosion. His intention to rebuild the factory and start over again, however, provoked a storm of protest from the frightened townspeople, who feared another explosion. When they refused to grant

Emil, the youngest Nobel brother, died in an explosion on September 3, 1864.

Nobel a permit to build a new plant in Heleneborg, he set up a factory on a large barge moored in the middle of a lake outside of the town. Two years later, in 1866, he moved to a factory in Germany.

Systematically, Nobel now began to look for some stable substance to mix with the nitroglycerin to make it safe to handle. He tried all sorts of materials—paper pulp, silica, sawdust, coal, ground charcoal, clay, and gypsum bars. Some of the combinations became lumpy and others would not absorb the nitroglycerin. Some did absorb the nitroglycerin but failed to explode properly.

Then one day in 1866, Nobel felt the lightweight, spongy material that the packers used to separate the cans of blasting oil in the shipping crates. Known as *kieselguhr* earth, the material had been formed over a period of millions of years by huge deposits of fossils. Because it was both loose and porous, Nobel decided to try it.

To his great satisfaction, the *kieselguhr* soaked up the nitroglycerin like a sponge, resulting in a putty-like substance. Nobel found he could knead the material into any shape he wanted. He could form it into sticks that would fit into the blasting holes bored into rock. Excited, Nobel began to test the safety of nitroglycerin mixed with the *kieselguhr* earth. After many experiments, he determined it was impossible to detonate the explosive by accident. With a blasting cap as the detonator, the sticks exploded with almost the same power as the pure nitroglycerin. Nobel had achieved his goal of a safe product.

Not wanting to use the now-tarnished name of nitroglycerin, Nobel looked for a new name for the explosive. With his knowledge of languages, he thought of the Greek word for power—*dynamis*—and decided to call his new invention dynamite. It became the invention for which Nobel is best known.

After Nobel demonstrated dynamite's effectiveness, ease of handling, and safety, it was used by engineers, geologists, and farmers to change the face of the earth. As engineers cut roads and tunnels through mountains, dynamite revolutionized transportation. As geologists dug into the earth, dynamite unlocked deposits of minerals such as copper, iron, zinc, lead, silver, and gold. As farmers and city planners developed land, dynamite removed obstructions. Other industries also found a multitude of uses for this amazing product.

By 1873, when Nobel was 40 years old, he had factories throughout the world. Nobel now traveled the globe, marketing his products, opening plants, and overseeing production. He spent such long periods abroad that he had no permanent home, commenting, "My homeland is wherever I'm working, and I work everywhere." After years of hard work, Alfred Nobel was a wealthy man.

A perfectionist, Nobel continued with his experiments. He wanted to improve the power of his invention even further. In 1875, he developed a new explosive in the form of a blasting gelatin, which he named gelignite,

In the 1880s, the dangerous Hellgate rocks that had blocked the New York City harbor were spectacularly removed by dynamite, which worked underwater as well as on land.

sometimes called "super dynamite." Nobel now had the perfect explosive. Even more powerful than pure nitroglycerin, gelignite was insensitive to shock and resistant to moisture.

As his wealth increased, Nobel decided to settle down. He bought an elegant mansion in Paris, where he installed a laboratory to continue with his experiments.

Like his brothers in Russia, Nobel also became interested in armaments.

In the 1880s, several European governments were searching for a new explosive to replace ordinary black gunpowder, which had one distinct drawback: choking,

Seventeen-year-old Alfred Nobel (left) pictured with his older brother Ludvig. In 1879, Alfred joined Ludvig and their brother Robert to form the Branobel Company. Robert had staked out a claim on the rich Baku oil fields in Russia. By the turn of the century, the oil produced by their company exceeded the entire U.S. output. Alfred helped design pipelines that carried the oil to a harbor on the Caspian Sea.

blinding black smoke. Experimenting to develop a smokeless high explosive for warfare, Nobel produced a substance that he named ballistite. Smokeless, easily stored, and inexpensive, ballistite was also more powerful than gunpowder.

In 1887, Nobel offered ballistite to the French gunpowder monopoly. Because the group of companies had already accepted a similar product from one of its own researchers, the monopoly rejected the offer. Nobel then took his invention to the Italian government, which accepted ballistite. Immediately, the French press accused Nobel of stealing secrets from the monopoly's research laboratories, and they labeled him a traitor. The French government withdrew Nobel's licenses for firearms and forbade him to manufacture ballistite in France.

Feeling both angry and betrayed, Nobel left France and moved to Italy. For a time, he worked on various substitutes for natural raw materials, pioneering the manufacture of artificial rubber, leather, and silk. He was never without ideas. "If I have a thousand ideas a year," he said, "and only one turns out to be good, I'm satisfied."

As the years passed, lawsuits, public derision, and a lack of acceptance plagued Nobel, who was becoming increasingly troubled by the destructive capabilities of his inventions. Yet he continued to believe that his efforts to create the ultimate deterrent would finally end war. "The day when two army corps can annihilate one another in a second," he stated, "all civilized nations, it is to be hoped,

*Alfred Nobel's villa at San Remo, Italy, on the coast
of the Mediterranean Sea, just across the border from
France. Described as "the wealthiest vagabond in
Europe," Nobel never had a permanent home or
family of his own.*

will recoil from war and discharge their troops." Above
all, Nobel wanted to be remembered as a man of peace.

When Nobel's brother Ludvig died in 1888, a news-
paper obituary confused the two and referred to Alfred as
the "the merchant of death." This shocking epithet
deeply troubled him. Seven years later, he wrote his final
will to reflect his strong commitment to peace.

In his will, Nobel outlined his intentions, directing
his executors to interpret and implement them. After
bequests to a few family members and employees, he left

the bulk of his 33 million Swedish kroner estate (more than $9 million at the time) to provide for an interest-producing fund, with the interest "annually distributed in the form of prizes to those who, during the preceding year, shall have conferred the greatest benefit on mankind."

Nobel further directed that the prize money was to be divided into five parts, or prizes: physics, chemistry, physiology or medicine, literature, and peace. He stipulated that a committee in Norway was to award the Peace Prize, while the other four prizes were to be awarded in Sweden. (A prize for economics was added in 1968 and was first awarded the following year.)

On December 10, 1896, a year after writing his will, Alfred Nobel died of a cerebral hemorrhage he had suffered three days before. His life ended much as he had lived—alone—with no relatives or close friends to comfort him in his final hours.

Newspapers heralded Alfred Nobel's will as the most magnificent gift of its kind ever made by a private person. But many people raised objections to the document. Some doubted the ability of the executors to set up the necessary organizations to implement it, and various relatives felt they should control the funds. The king of Sweden objected to Norway being involved. It took three years for the executors to deal with the objections and to set up the necessary legal documents. Finally, on June 29, 1900, the Swedish government approved the statutes needed to carry out Nobel's wishes.

Subsequently, the Nobel Foundation was established in Sweden, and the Nobel Institute was created to administer and distribute the four prizes given there. Ragnar Sohlman, an engineer who had worked for Nobel in San Remo and had helped settle the dispute over Nobel's will, was appointed executive director of the foundation. In Norway, a similar institute was formed to administer the Nobel Peace Prize.

Bertha von Suttner (1843-1914) was employed briefly as Nobel's secretary in 1875. She later became a tireless advocate for world peace and wrote Lay Down Your Arms!, *a book that was widely read upon its publication in 1889. Von Suttner influenced Nobel's thinking and convinced him to attend an International Peace Congress in 1892. In 1905, Bertha von Suttner received the Nobel Peace Prize.*

Ever since, Nobel prize winners have been chosen by committees that are appointed to review hundreds of prospects over a 10-month period. They consult with renowned leaders in their respective fields throughout the world to determine those who have earned the right to be named Nobel laureates. Each year's winners are announced to the press in October, two months prior to the award ceremonies.

As stipulated by Nobel, the prizes are open to all individuals—regardless of gender, nationality, race, or ideology—and they may be divided among two or three recipients. Only the Peace Prize can be awarded to an institution. In some years, the various prizes have been withheld, usually because of an existing global conflict. For example, the Peace Prize was not given from 1939 to 1943 during some of the years of World War II.

Since 1901, women and men throughout the world have received the Nobel Prizes—the highest distinction that humanity bestows upon one of its own. The awards are presented at impressive ceremonies on December 10 each year—the Peace Prize in Oslo and the others in Stockholm. The legacy left by Alfred Nobel has given the world a long list of illustrious laureates, people whose great achievements have made and continue to make the world a better place.

In 1901, physicist Wilhelm Roentgen (1845-1923) was the first recipient of the Nobel Prize for his discovery of X rays. Since that time, only two people have been awarded the Nobel Prize in two different fields. Marie Curie (1867-1934) won her first prize in physics in 1903 and the chemistry prize eight years later. Linus Pauling (1901-1994), below, received the chemistry prize in 1954 and the peace prize in 1962.

*Cecil John Rhodes (1853-1902) left the fortune he
had amassed to his alma mater. "Wherever you turn
your eye," he wrote, "an Oxford man is at the top of
the tree."*

2

Cecil John Rhodes
Diamonds and Dreams

*I*n 1992, voters in the United States elected a Rhodes scholar as their president. While Rhodes scholars count among their number some of the world's ablest leaders, Bill Clinton was the first to run for—and to win—the highest office in the United States. Cecil Rhodes, the political leader, financier, and dreamer who established the Rhodes scholarships at Oxford University, would have been proud. More than anything, Rhodes wanted his scholars to be leaders and to make meaningful contributions to improve the world.

A Rhodes Scholarship is considered one of the world's most prestigious academic honors. To be awarded the privilege of two years of study at Oxford University in England, applicants must meet stringent requirements. Along with intellectual and academic achievement, the selection committee looks for leadership ability and integrity of character.

Cecil Rhodes himself probably would not have qualified for such a scholarship. As a student, he did not display the intellect or ability required to win this distinguished award. But he fantasized about forming a secret society of the most able men in the English-speaking world who would be dedicated to improving the world and eliminating war.

Cecil John Rhodes was born into a large family on July 5, 1853, in the town of Bishop Stortford, England, in the countryside north of London. His father, Francis Rhodes, the vicar of St. Michael's Church, was a stern and domineering man. Cecil felt closer to his mother, Louisa Peacock Rhodes.

Expecting to go to a university as his older brothers had done, Cecil wanted to study law at Oxford. When the time came for him to enter college, however, his poor health, along with a shortage of family funds, forced a change of plans. Instead of college, his father sent him to South Africa to join his brother, Herbert, who needed help on his cotton farm. His father also believed that Cecil's health would benefit from the mild climate there.

Rhodes was disappointed to have to delay his Oxford education, but he was excited about this new adventure. He sailed in late June 1870, just before his seventeenth birthday, and arrived in Durban 72 days later.

South Africa was a very different country in 1870 than it is today. Then it was a hodgepodge of vast territories. The British ruled the Cape Colony on the southern coast and Natal on the east coast. Descendants of the Dutch, who had settled in South Africa two centuries before, had established two Boer (the Dutch word for farmer) republics in the north, the Transvaal and the Orange Free State. The huge expanses of the interior were populated by African tribes.

In 1869, the year before Cecil Rhodes arrived, a native African farm worker had found a large, bright stone lying on the ground. Deciding to sell it to a man known to be a buyer of pretty stones, the farm hand received his asking price of 500 sheep, 10 oxen, and a horse!

The "pretty stone" turned out to be one of the largest diamonds ever found, an amazing 83 carats. Named the Star of Africa, it passed through several hands and was eventually sold in England for £25,000 (about $120,000 at the time). Subsequently, other farmers and native Africans in the area discovered diamonds on several large farms and in riverbeds.

The news of riches to be found by digging in the ground lured hundreds, then thousands, of fortune seekers to South Africa. They rushed to buy or rent small plots of land, staking out their claims. Like prospecting California gold after 1849, digging for diamonds was an irresistible attraction. Diamond mining would set the stage for dramatic changes in South Africa, and Cecil Rhodes would play a key role in those changes.

When Cecil arrived in Natal, he found his brother had impetuously left his cotton farm for the newly discovered diamond fields. Although Herbert, having no luck in the difficult work of mining diamonds, returned to the farm in time for the harvest, the brothers' first crop was a complete failure.

After replanting, Herbert returned to the diamond fields, leaving 18-year-old Cecil in charge of the farm and 30 laborers. This responsibility did much for the young Rhodes's self-esteem. In a letter to his mother, he wrote that "I am left in charge here and . . . feel quite a big man."

Cecil was certain that the cotton crop would bring him the money he needed to realize his dream of attending Oxford. Instead, the crop brought a poor price at market. Discouraged with farming, Cecil decided to make the 400-mile journey to join Herbert, who by then had staked out several diamond claims.

In 1871, when Cecil arrived in New Rush (soon to be known as Kimberley), he was astounded by the incredible frenzy of "diamond fever." Writing to his mother, he described the mine as an immense number of ant heaps covered with working ants who were really humans.

*In the 1870s, the Kimberley mine was a labyrinth of
workers, wires, wagons, tools, and sometimes—to those
who successfully negotiated the mining maze—diamonds.*

Several weeks after Cecil arrived, Herbert left for
new adventures in the Transvaal, selling his claims in
Kimberley to his brother. Rhodes observed the mining
scene growing more and more chaotic. With the owners
of hundreds of small claims searching and digging, the
Kimberley diamond field became one huge, deep hole in
the ground. Around the mine, hastily built roads crum-
bled. Diamonds were stolen, then traded illegally, causing
the market price of all diamonds to fluctuate wildly.

At first, Rhodes considered diamond mining to be only a gamble, but he soon realized that diamonds could become an important industry if they were put under some kind of control. As Rhodes watched the miners laboriously bringing up loads of earth to sort through for brilliant stones, he thought about how to end the confusion. If he bought up enough claims and consolidated them into a large holding, he could regulate diamond

A lunch break from digging diamonds at J. Dick-Lauder's camp, in the early 1870s. Herbert Rhodes (center) stands behind his brother, Cecil.

pricing, stop the thievery, and organize the industry. With consolidation and organization, Rhodes could change the gamble to a sure thing, bringing him wealth and power.

During this time, Rhodes developed a lifelong friendship with a young man named Charles Dunell Rudd. Like Rhodes, Rudd had come to South Africa to recuperate from an illness. Together they formed a partnership in mining and other speculative ventures, including ice making. Although the partners realized some short-term profits from their other ventures, nothing succeeded like their diamond-mining enterprise.

By the summer of 1873, Rhodes was worth about £10,000 ($48,000)—money he had earned from the diamond claims sold to him by his brother. Anxious to finally realize his long-held dream of enrolling at Oxford, Rhodes left his partner in charge of the lucrative claims and set sail for England.

Rhodes liked to boast that he had "sent himself up to Oxford," a difficult accomplishment in those days when a student needed family sponsorship. Oxford had requirements in Greek and Latin that Rhodes was unable to meet to earn an honors degree, but he was accepted for a lower degree in October 1873. After just one term, Rhodes suffered a heart attack. His poor health, along with pressing problems at the diggings, forced him to return to Kimberley. It would be three years before he could again leave South Africa to resume his education at Oxford University.

*Cecil Rhodes as
a 24-year-old
undergraduate
student at
Oriel College,
Oxford*

In 1874, problems at the mine began with uncontrolled competition among the diggers. Then, as levels of digging reached a depth of 80 feet, the geological make-up of the earth changed. The soft, yellow ground, which had yielded diamonds, gave way to hard, blue-colored ground that was much more difficult to work. Discouraged, scores of diggers gave up their claims because they assumed there were no more diamonds to be found in the blue ground.

Rhodes now seized the opportunity to acquire the large holdings he had wanted. He guessed that new and improved methods could be developed to work the blue ground, with even greater yields. As the miners left, Rhodes and his partner cheaply bought up all the available claims.

In 1876, the Rhodes-Rudd business partnership expanded even further when the two men began to buy up claims on the large farms owned by the two De Beers brothers. Within four years, the partners had acquired most of the remaining large diamond claims on the two huge farms and established the De Beers Mining Company. The growth and success of their new company demonstrated the effectiveness of having a large organization control the mining.

While building his business, Rhodes shuttled between England and Africa. Rudd managed the business whenever Rhodes was pursuing his studies. In 1881, eight years after he had begun, Rhodes received his bachelor of arts degree. He was certain that an Oxford education would enable him to be a better businessman and would also provide him with the key to power and greatness.

At Oxford, Rhodes pondered the meaning of his life. Because of his continual health problems, he began to feel his life would be short. In 1877, he decided to put his dreams and ideas into a document—a final will and testament—which he called "Confessions of Faith." Although much of what he wrote was rambling and not fully developed, Rhodes felt the concepts expressed in his document were inspired and brilliant.

Rhodes believed the chief goal of his life should be to render himself useful to Great Britain, his native country. He felt that British rule throughout the world would improve life everywhere and could even eliminate war. He fantasized about forming a secret society with the goal of extending British rule and even bringing the United States back into the British Empire.

To accomplish his objective of developing South Africa for the British Empire, Cecil Rhodes realized he would need great wealth. Nine years after writing his "Confessions," he found a way to acquire that wealth. In 1886, with the help of his business advisor, Alfred Beit, who obtained the necessary financial backing, Rhodes bought the remaining shares of the lucrative Kimberley mine from his largest competitor, Barney Barnato. With this purchase, Rhodes formed an even larger company, De Beers Consolidated Mines. This acquisition fulfilled Rhodes's ambition to make De Beers "the richest, the greatest, and the most powerful company the world has ever seen." Rhodes now controlled all the mines in Kimberley, which contained more than 90 percent of the world's diamonds.

The next year, in 1887, Rhodes became even wealthier when the world's richest source of gold was discovered in nearby Transvaal. Rhodes moved into the gold fields to make a second fortune. This venture provided him with an enormous income and huge assets worth twice what he had gained from diamonds.

With the attainment of his two dreams—an Oxford education and great wealth—Rhodes now turned to fulfilling his goal of developing South Africa. Seven years earlier, in 1880, he had entered the arena of politics and had been elected to a lifetime seat in the parliament of the Cape Colony. This position gave Rhodes a base of authority to develop South Africa as much for himself as for Queen Victoria and the British Empire.

Now that Rhodes was no longer traveling between Oxford and Kimberley, he turned his time and energy

The Cape Legislative Assembly in the late 1880s. Rhodes is seated in the first row on the left side, second from the wall.

43

toward expanding British South Africa to the north. He knew that both farmers and miners were suffering from the lack of transportation there and that an addition to the railroad between Cape Town and Kimberley needed to be built to reach the newly discovered gold-bearing areas in the Transvaal. The only feasible route for the new railway was through Bechuanaland (now Botswana), a vast tribal state on the northern border of the Cape Colony. With Rhodes as a key political figure to negotiate treaties with the tribal chiefs who occupied the land, Bechuanaland became a British possession in 1885. This agreement guaranteed that the railway system could now be extended northward.

In 1890, Rhodes became prime minister of the Cape Colony. This office gave him the power to establish the program that he favored for a strong South African economy under British control. He further improved the railroad system, adding thousands of miles of track, and opened new seaports to increase overseas trade. He created the first ministry of agriculture and, with the use of technology and tariffs, made farming more successful. To maintain British white rule effectively, Rhodes supported the Glen Gray Act that assigned specific living areas for the African natives. Eventually, this led to *apartheid*, which means apartness in Afrikaans, the Boer language. Although this system of racial segregation and white supremacy caused international protest and domestic unrest, apartheid laws were not repealed until 1991.

In the 1880s, a rivalry developed among some European nations for African territory. Great Britain, Portugal, and Germany established charter companies to acquire valuable territory from tribal rulers. European colonists settled large areas, extracting or using natural resources, which permanently altered the political and economic structures of native African peoples.

On October 29, 1889, the British government granted Rhodes a charter to incorporate the British South Africa Company. With this official backing of the British government, Rhodes was able to establish his own private colonization venture. In 1894, the territory that now makes up the independent nations of Zimbabwe and Zambia became the country of Rhodesia.

During the years between 1890 and 1895, Rhodes became an international figure who was admired at home and abroad for his accomplishments in South Africa. On his yearly visits to England, he was entertained by Queen Victoria and others in high society. On the streets, cabbies shouted greetings of recognition.

By 1895, Rhodes had reached the pinnacle of his political career. Yet he had not reached his goal of uniting all of southern Africa for the British Empire. As his heart weakened, he was afraid his poor health would deny him the time he needed to attain this dream.

To hasten things along, Rhodes decided to interfere in the politics of the Transvaal, the area occupied by the Dutch descendants known as Boers or Afrikaners.

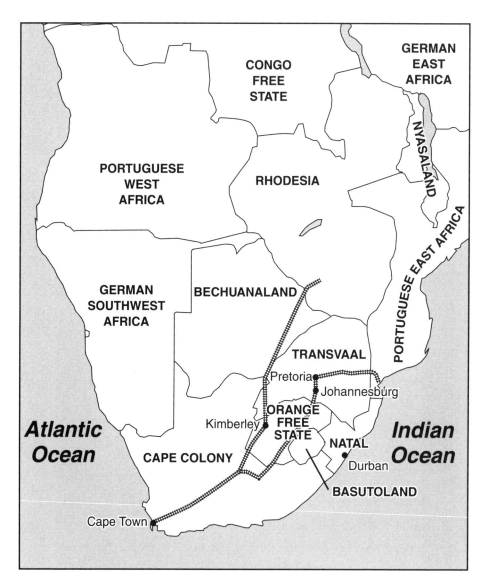

GERMAN
EAST
AFRICA

CONGO
FREE
STATE

NYASALAND

PORTUGUESE
WEST
AFRICA

RHODESIA

GERMAN
SOUTHWEST
AFRICA

BECHUANALAND

PORTUGUESE EAST AFRICA

TRANSVAAL

Pretoria

Johannesburg

Atlantic
Ocean

Kimberley

ORANGE
FREE
STATE

NATAL

Indian
Ocean

CAPE COLONY

Durban

BASUTOLAND

Cape Town

The political boundaries of southern Africa at the
height of Cecil Rhodes's power in 1895

46

Their president, Paul Kruger, wanted "Africa for the Afrikaners," but Rhodes wanted southern Africa for the British. He sought to bring the Transvaal under British jurisdiction and, with the approval of the British colonial secretary, backed an invasion of the Boer republic to over-throw the government of President Kruger.

Led by Rhodes's representative, Leander Starr Jameson, the 1895 raid failed when a planned uprising by British immigrants in the area failed to materialize. The Boers jailed Jameson for leading the raid, while Rhodes, criticized by the public for his part, resigned his post as prime minister of the Cape Colony. Named for its leader, the Jameson Raid increased the friction between the British settlers and the Boers. Tensions escalated four years later, and the Boer War broke out in 1899. By 1902, the British had gained control of the territory they sought.

The Jameson Raid tarnished Rhodes's reputation and diminished his political influence. Rhodes spent the final years of his life traveling back and forth between England and South Africa. His main thoughts and activity involved his will. Finally, his diseased heart gave out, and he died on March 26, 1902.

Cecil Rhodes, the businessman who wanted to turn his dreams into reality, had hoped for a place in history. In his short life, he did more than any other individual to influence the British colonization and development of South Africa, both economically and politically. Many

After the Boers captured Leander Starr Jameson (1853–1917), they sent him back to London where he was tried and sentenced to 15 months in prison. Following his release, Jameson returned to South Africa and served as the colony's premier from 1904 to 1908.

people also believe that in the process, Rhodes helped to destroy the native African tribal societies.

Today, however, Rhodes is best remembered for his legacy of £6 million (over $29 million) that established scholarships at his cherished Oxford University. In his will, Rhodes outlined the requirements for his scholarships. A board of trustees would be appointed and given the authority to decide who would qualify. The scholarships were to be awarded to students from countries that were a part of the British Empire—Canada, Australia, New Zealand, India, and Pakistan—as well as Germany and the United States.

Strong objections arose when the terms of Rhodes's will became known to the governing body at Oxford. How could the Rhodes trustees usurp the university's decisions about who should study at Oxford? The officials of that exclusive university worried about the influx of nearly 200 new students each year from countries where educational standards might not be as high as in Great Britain. They even objected to the use of the word "scholar." Fortunately, Rhodes had given his trustees considerable leeway in making decisions to implement the plan and, although it took two years, the trustees and the university authorities did reach an agreement.

Today, committees established in 18 English-speaking countries select scholars based on academic achievement, integrity, leadership, and athletic ability. There are no racial barriers to the two-year scholarships, and women have been eligible since 1976.

The scholarships have given thousands of outstanding students a unique educational opportunity. Rhodes scholars have gone on to excel in many fields of endeavor, including education, law, economics, public service, entertainment, and business—just as their benefactor had intended.

Andrew Carnegie (1835-1919) began working at age 13 to help support his family. Fifty-three years later, he was the richest man in the world.

3

Andrew Carnegie
Prince of Steel

A ndrew Carnegie was the first philanthropist to state publicly that the rich have a moral obligation to distribute their fortunes for the general good. In his 1889 essay, "Gospel of Wealth," Carnegie asserted that all personal wealth beyond that required for the needs of one's family should be regarded as a trust fund for the benefit of the community.

True to his beliefs, when Andrew Carnegie died at the age of 83, he had given away the bulk of his $480 million fortune.

The Carnegie family lived on the second floor of this small cottage in Dunfermline, Scotland. The workroom where Andrew's father sat at his loom, weaving linens by hand, was on the first floor.

Andrew Carnegie started life in Dunfermline, Scotland, on November 25, 1835, the first son born to William and Margaret Morrison Carnegie. Another son, Thomas, was born eight years later. Before Andrew started school at the age of eight, he was educated by his father and his uncle, George Lauder. Roaming the countryside of his beloved Scotland with his uncle, Andrew learned about the wonders of nature, as well as history and literature. Watching his father weave, Andrew absorbed the values of hard work and individual enterprise.

The family thrived until the mid-1840s, when factories with faster and more efficient power looms put hand weavers such as William out of work. Proud and stubborn, he refused to work in the linen factory, choosing instead to sit by his loom, waiting for orders that never came.

With little money, life had became desperate for the Carnegies by the winter of 1847. Urged by relatives who had already emigrated to the United States, Margaret decided that the family should go to America. The Carnegie family left Scotland in May 1848 and reached Allegheny, Pennsylvania, after a difficult three-month journey by sea and land.

In their new country, the Carnegies needed money to live. Instead of attending school, Andrew went to work as a bobbin boy in a thread factory. Just 13 years old, he worked 12 hours a day, six days out of seven, to earn a weekly wage of $1.20.

Factory work was difficult and tedious. So when Andrew learned about a job opening at the local telegraph office, he seized the opportunity. He and several other young boys were hired to deliver incoming messages to local businesses. (In 1849, the telegraph was an important new form of communication. Transmitting messages along the wires over long distances changed the way people did business.) Andrew's salary as a telegraph runner was $2.50 per week—more than twice what he had earned at the factory.

Ambitious and self-directed, Andrew soon picked up the dots and dashes of Morse code, tapping out simple messages to other offices. In fact, he became proficient enough to write down the messages as fast as they came in. Thus, he bypassed the slower method of translating the code from the telegraph machine's printed tape used by other operators. Because of his special skill, Andrew's employers raised his salary to $25 a month—remarkable wages for a 16-year-old boy with a limited education.

After Andrew had worked for three years in the telegraph office, he was offered a job by Thomas Scott, the superintendent of the Pittsburgh division of the Pennsylvania Railroad Company. In the early days of railroads, trains traveling in opposite directions had to share one track. When one train approached another, one of them had to be directed to move to a *siding*, or a side track, to let the other pass. In his new job, Carnegie sent messages by telegraph from station to station between Philadelphia and Pittsburgh to control the flow of traffic and keep the trains moving swiftly and safely.

Soon Carnegie became Scott's valued assistant, working at his side to investigate and solve problems in the field. When Scott advanced to vice-president of the Pennsylvania Railroad Company, Carnegie replaced him as superintendent of the Pittsburgh division. With his salary now raised to $125 per month, Carnegie settled his newly widowed mother and his brother in a modest house in a Pittsburgh suburb.

Carnegie's promotion put him into a community of people who valued achievement, not family background or formal education. Wanting to fit in, he began to pay attention to the way he talked and dressed, and he worked to acquire social graces. Carnegie liked to associate with learned and literate people and, being well-read, he enjoyed discussing the issues of the day. He was, for example, against the practice of slavery that was threatening to split the Union, and he expressed his views on social and political conditions by writing essays and sending them to newspapers for publication.

In 1856, Scott loaned Carnegie $600 to invest in a growing company, Adams Express. Carnegie's first *dividend,* or profit, from his share as an investing partner was $10. Amazed and delighted, he exclaimed, "I shall remember that check as long as I live! It gave me the first penny of revenue . . . that I had not worked for with the sweat of my brow. 'Eureka!' I cried. 'Here's the goose that lays the golden eggs.'"

During his years with the railroad, Carnegie took advantage of several other investment opportunities in such industries as oil, bridges, rails, locomotives, and iron mills. He relied on his intuition to buy into companies that were important to the future growth of the United States. One such venture was the Woodruff Sleeping Car Company, which later merged with the Pullman Company. Carnegie predicted that railroad expansion would result in longer trips, and he was certain that passengers would want to use the new railway car with beds and washrooms. This successful investment prompted Carnegie to say, "Blessed is the man who invented sleep." The venture was the beginning of Carnegie's fortune.

By 1865, Carnegie realized he was making more money from his investments in other companies than from his salary as a railroad employee, so he resigned. To gain majority control of his companies, he bought out some of his other partners. Carnegie liked the idea of being "my own master, manufacturing something and giving employment to many men."

By the age of 33, Carnegie had an annual income of $50,000 per year from his investments. (This amount would equal approximately $750,000 in 1997.) Going over his financial records, he wrote himself the following memo: "Beyond this never earn—make no effort to increase fortune, but spend the surplus each year for benevolent purposes."

By 1870, almost everything Carnegie's companies made—bridges, railroad tracks, locomotives, and sleeping cars—all depended on iron. For at least 3,000 years, iron had been manufactured by throwing measured quantities of iron ore, coke (a carbon residue), and limestone into a large blast furnace. Blasts of hot air were then forced into the burning mixture, and a relatively pure iron was released from the ore through a chemical reaction.

But iron had its limitations. Railroad tracks manu-factured from iron quickly wore out, requiring frequent replacement. In 1856, the search for a harder metal led to the development of a new refining process. Sir Henry Bessemer (1813-1898) of England invented a converter through which molten pig iron flowed, with manganese and other materials added. The refined iron became known as steel.

Carnegie waited to see if the steel produced by this method could compete with iron. He met with Bessemer in England in 1872 to observe his furnace in action. Bessemer's converter not only produced a more durable metal, but also proved more efficient than iron furnaces. Carnegie rushed back to America to tell his associates, "The day of iron has passed. Steel is king!"

In 1873, Carnegie built a steel mill to concentrate on large-scale steel production using the Bessemer process. Built outside of Pittsburgh, he named his plant the Edgar Thompson Works after the head of the Pennsylvania Railroad. The mill integrated all the steps of steel pro-duction—from raw iron ore to the finished steel railroad tracks—and became a model for the steel industry.

In the same year that Carnegie constructed his steel mill, the financial Panic of 1873 began with the bank-ruptcy of the Northern Pacific Railroad, which set off a chain reaction of bank closings and business failures. The United States entered a depression that lasted for four years. With his companies on solid foundations, Carnegie maintained his faith in the country's ability to recover by continuing to build and expand. When the depression ended in 1877, Carnegie's companies were stronger than ever, and he was even richer than before.

After the depression, Carnegie spent his time immersed in building both his business empire and his personal fortune. His business connections were strengthened by his talent for dealing with people honestly and with good humor. In 1881, Carnegie decided to consolidate all his companies into one giant corporation, Carnegie Brothers & Company Ltd., the largest company of its kind in the United States. His new company

The Carnegie steel works in Farrel, Pennsylvania, one of the many mills in Carnegie's empire

In 1881, Andrew Carnegie fulfilled a promise made to his mother when he was just a young man. On a visit to Scotland, he hired this grand carriage to drive them into Dunfermline because Carnegie wanted his mother to return to her hometown in style.

handled virtually every component of steel manufacturing, from the extraction of raw iron to the finished product. Andrew put his brother, Tom, in charge of running the company.

One of the raw materials Carnegie needed to make steel was *coke*, a hard substance of almost pure carbon that was produced from burning soft coal in special ovens. Carnegie bought his coke (derived from the word coal-cake) from another giant of American industry, Henry Clay Frick, who owned many of the rich coal fields in Pennsylvania. In 1883, Carnegie formed a partnership with Frick, guaranteeing a supply of coke for the Carnegie mills at a good price. Three years later, following the death of his brother, Tom, Carnegie put Frick in charge of all the Carnegie works, including the recently acquired steel mill at Homestead, Pennsylvania.

Carnegie's mother also died in 1886, a few weeks following Tom's death. Soon afterward, Carnegie became engaged to a young woman 21 years his junior. Louise Whitfield and Andrew Carnegie were married the next year, and the couple spent their honeymoon in Dunfermline. To Carnegie's delight, his new wife was so taken with Scotland that she insisted on spending their summers there. After the birth of their only child, Margaret, Carnegie purchased and renovated Skibo Castle near Dornoch Firth, Scotland, for the family to enjoy. Happily married, Carnegie spent less time at his plants.

During the latter years of the nineteenth century, factory employees began to speak out—and sometimes to strike—against long hours, low wages, child labor, and unsafe conditions. Carnegie was more advanced in his thinking than were most industrialists of his day. His workers generally earned good wages and could afford their own homes. Although he had publicly stated his support of the workers' right to join together, privately Carnegie and Henry Frick agreed that the Amalgamated Association of Iron and Steel Workers was growing too strong.

When a strike occurred at the Homestead plant during July 1892, Carnegie was in Scotland. Frick was in charge and hired replacement workers, along with 300 guards to protect them. His action sparked a bloody riot that ended with the deaths of nine people and injuries to many more. The state militia, called in by the governor of Pennsylvania, arrested the strike leaders and town officials on charges of riot and murder. The militia then reopened the steel plant to the replacement workers.

A few weeks after the Homestead strike, Henry Clay Frick (1849-1919) was shot twice by a young man who burst into Frick's office. The assailant, Alexander Berkman, sympathized with but was not a union member. Berkman was disarmed and arrested. Frick recovered from his wounds.

Although Carnegie was in Scotland during the Homestead strike, he was blamed for the company's actions because he had agreed with Frick about fighting the union. There are no records to indicate that Carnegie had approved of Frick's methods. Whether or not he had agreed to the tactics, Carnegie felt the tragedy was a stain on his good reputation.

Andrew Carnegie was ready to retire when, in 1901, J. P. Morgan, a powerful financier, offered to buy Carnegie's entire iron and steel empire for whatever price Carnegie asked. Carnegie took a sheet of paper and wrote $480 million. When Morgan met Carnegie to shake

Under the ownership of John Pierpont Morgan (1837-1913), the Carnegie steel mills became the U.S. Steel Corporation, the first billion-dollar company in the world.

hands on the deal a few days later, he turned to Carnegie and said, "I want to congratulate you on being the richest man in the world."

Now Carnegie faced the task of deciding how to distribute his millions. Intending to live by his philosophy that "to die rich is to die disgraced," he began to give away large sums of money through personal gifts and the establishment of various trusts. Because he wanted to improve people's lives and do away with ignorance, he used his money to construct libraries, parks, art galleries, theaters, hospitals, and other public facilities.

Carnegie is probably best known for building free public libraries. Before he promoted the public library system that still exists today, most libraries were private and charged a user's fee. Carnegie gave money to more than 2,500 communities in the English-speaking world for libraries, and many buildings still bear his name.

Carnegie took as much pleasure in giving away his fortune as he had in making it. In Pittsburgh, he founded the Carnegie Institute in 1895 and endowed the Carnegie Institute of Technology in 1900. These schools are now part of Carnegie-Mellon University. In 1902, he established the Carnegie Institution of Washington, D.C., a center for scientific research, primarily in the fields of astronomy, biology, and earth sciences. In 1904, he formed the Carnegie Hero Fund Commission to recognize everyday acts of heroism in the United States and Canada. Probably Carnegie's most personal cause, the

This Carnegie library in Austin, Minnesota, is typical of the hundreds of libraries Carnegie donated to towns all across America. To apply for a library, a town council had to provide a building site and pledge an annual appropriation for books and maintenance, which was usually 10 percent of the Carnegie gift.

commission remains in existence today. The fund honors people who risked or sacrificed their lives to save (or attempt to save) the life of another person.

In 1905, Carnegie endowed the Carnegie Foundation for the Advancement of Teaching for the study of education policy. Five years later, he created the Carnegie Endowment for International Peace to educate the

American public about the complexities of international problems and to hasten the end of war.

Despite his many *benefactions*, or charitable gifts, Carnegie realized he was not giving his money away fast enough. So in 1911, he established a foundation, the Carnegie Corporation, with the mission "to promote the advancement and diffusion of knowledge and understanding." Funding the corporation with $135 million, Carnegie gave the trustees full authority to change its policy when necessary or desirable. He realized that "conditions upon the earth inevitably change: hence, no wise man will bind Trustees forever to certain paths, causes, or institutions."

Today, with assets over $1 billion, the Carnegie Corporation concentrates its numerous activities on social justice, equality, and human resource development. Dedicated to helping children, the corporation works to solve the problems of disadvantaged youth. It sponsors the educational television program "Sesame Street" and also funds studies to find ways of improving public schools.

Andrew Carnegie died at his home in Lenox, Massachusetts, on August 11, 1919. In the years since his death, the organizations that he founded have grown beyond anything he might have imagined. As America's first great philanthropist, Andrew Carnegie demonstrated how wealth generously given and wisely spent can improve the lives of others.

*At one point during his life, John Davison Rockefeller
(1839-1937) was called the most hated man in
America because of his ruthless business practices. But
his many charitable gifts and the foundation he
established have created a legacy of generosity.*

4

John D. Rockefeller
Standard Oil Tycoon

*J*ohn D. Rockefeller was only 10 years old when he executed his first business deal. He had saved $50 from money he earned hoeing potatoes for a wage of 34 cents a day. When the farmer who employed him needed to borrow $50, John loaned the man the money, charging him 7 percent interest. A year later, when the farmer repaid the loan, John received $3.50 in interest—more than he could have made working in the potato fields for 10 days! He gave 10 percent of his profit to charity and saved the rest.

John learned about money from his father, William Avery Rockefeller. Known as "Big Bill," William Rockefeller was an amiable man who taught his three sons how to be clever in business and how to buy and sell to their advantage. Sometimes he loaned them money, charging 10 percent interest, and, in turn, paid the same rate when he borrowed from them. He instructed his sons to regard a business deal as a sacred contract.

John credited his father with giving him an appreciation for business, but it was his mother, Eliza Davison Rockefeller, who taught him the values of thrift and charity. She insisted John give a portion of his earnings to the Baptist Church, a practice he continued throughout his life.

John Davison Rockefeller was born on July 8, 1839, in Richford, New York, the second oldest of five children. After moving several times, the family settled near Cleveland, Ohio, where John attended high school. A serious student, he found most subjects difficult, but he loved math. John also enjoyed debating and developed the style of soft-spoken, persistent persuasion he would later use so effectively in business to bring others to his way of thinking.

After high school and a short business course in accounting and bookkeeping, 16-year-old John was ready to look for his first job. "I did not guess what it would be," he remembered. "But I was after something big." With good jobs difficult to find, he systematically called on every business firm in Cleveland. His persistence paid off when a commission house named Hewitt and Tuttle hired him to work as a bookkeeper. The date was September 26, 1855, a day that Rockefeller would celebrate as a holiday for the rest of his life.

In the mid-1800s, firms such as Hewitt and Tuttle acted as go-betweens in all forms of commerce. They put buyers and sellers of goods together, and then arranged for shipment and payment. For this, they earned a *commission*, or percentage of the sale. Rockefeller worked long hours at his job, learning about the commission business and business practices in general. After several years, he was ready to go into business for himself. He formed a partnership with an acquaintance, Maurice B. Clark, who had been working for another commission house.

In the new firm of Clark and Rockefeller, which opened for business in April 1859, John ran the office, kept the books, and negotiated the logistics of moving shipments of produce and goods. Maurice worked outside the office, traveling the countryside to obtain crops from farmers wanting to sell their produce. The farmers would *consign*, or turn over, their crops to Clark and Rockefeller to resell and ship for them. The partners made a profit if they sold these consignments for more money than they paid to the farmers.

To get ahead of the competition, Rockefeller used aggressive business practices. He would borrow money from banks to pay advances to the farmers for their crops before he found buyers for the goods. Farmers were willing to sell at a cheaper rate if they could receive a portion of their money before their crops were ready for harvest. This practice was risky for the partnership because selling prices could drop before they found buyers for their consignments. But Rockefeller's father had taught him the importance of borrowing needed cash in order to take advantage of a good deal.

The lesson paid off. During their first year in business, Clark and Rockefeller realized a profit of more than $4,000. By the next year, their profit was $17,000.

In his early twenties, John D. Rockefeller was already running a successful business, investing in promising stocks, and giving generously to his church.

While Rockefeller and Clark were finding success in the commission house business, a new industry rose from the ground. In 1859, Edwin L. Drake drilled the first oil well near Oil Creek, a stream in northwest Pennsylvania. In those days, 20 years before Thomas Edison had perfected the electric light bulb, lamps were lit with messy candles or with foul-smelling whale oil. Crude oil (petroleum) coming from the ground could be cheaply turned into kerosene, which was clean and relatively odorless. Lighting with kerosene became so popular and profitable that the precious oil came to be known as "black gold." The area near Titusville, Pennsylvania, was called the Oil Region and attracted swarms of fortune hunters.

In 1863, Samuel Andrews, a friend of Clark's, approached Clark and Rockefeller about joining a new company to refine oil. Andrews had developed an advanced and efficient method of *refining*, or removing impurities from the oil, but he had no business experience. Clark's brother, James, would also join the new partnership, which was known as Andrews, Clark and Company. Rockefeller invested $4,000.

As soon as he realized the potential profit in oil refining, Rockefeller became actively involved in the business. In this new venture, he continued his successful practice of borrowing money in order to expand and to compete, but the two Clark brothers became increasingly uneasy about the growing debt. Andrews, on the other hand, agreed with Rockefeller's business decisions.

Tensions increased until it was obvious that the partnership could not continue. In 1865, Rockefeller and Andrews bought out the Clark brothers and changed the company's name to Rockefeller and Andrews. Rockefeller referred to the purchase of this business as "the day that I determined my career." At age 26, he was ready to begin building an empire.

The year before, in 1864, Rockefeller had married a young woman he knew from high school. Laura Celestia Spelman returned to Cleveland to teach after attending college. "Cettie" was an independent young woman who believed in women's rights. Her parents were active in the movement to abolish slavery. She also shared John Rockefeller's interest in the Baptist Church. Rockefeller respected his wife's views and consulted with her about all his business dealings. He later said, "Her judgment was always better than mine. Without her keen advice I would be a poor man."

In the early days of drilling in the Oil Region, no one knew where producing wells would be found. This uncertainty caused prices to fluctuate wildly, creating chaos for the speculators. Rockefeller made numerous trips to meet with drill operators, refinery owners, and railroad executives. As he began to understand the potential of the oil industry, he also began to see himself as the person best suited to bring order to the existing confusion.

With his characteristic thoroughness, Rockefeller approached the problem logically. After deciding that

One of the many oil drilling rigs that dotted the landscape of northwest Pennsylvania after oil was discovered near Titusville in 1859

refining oil was more profitable than drilling for it, he formed his plan of action. Refineries already existed in the Oil Region, and also in Pittsburgh, New York, and Rockefeller's home city of Cleveland. To begin, Rockefeller intended to buy up all the refineries in Cleveland to eliminate any competition. Then he would arrange for economical storage and low-cost shipping in order to compete with the refineries located closer to the oil fields and the export markets.

To implement his plan, Rockefeller intended to gather able people around him who shared his vision.

He started by bringing his younger brother, William, into the business. He sent William to New York City to oversee the lucrative export market. (At that time, about 70 percent of refined oil was sent to overseas markets.)

Then Rockefeller hired Andrews's brother and sent him to the Oil Region in Pennsylvania to be ready to buy crude oil whenever the prices dropped, which was usually due to a surplus of oil. If needed, Rockefeller would borrow money to buy huge quantities of cheap crude to store in warehouses for future use.

All refineries used the railroads to ship oil, both crude and refined, but the railroads had to deal with erratic supplies of oil. At times, the railroads did not have enough cars to handle the heavy inventory; the next week, their cars might stand empty and idle in the yards.

The costs of shipping oil to and from Cleveland put Rockefeller at a disadvantage with his eastern competitors. In 1867, Rockefeller brought in a new partner, Henry Flagler, a dynamic and brilliant negotiator, to help him resolve this problem. Together, they made a favorable deal with the railroads—one that would use the railroads' problem to solve their own.

With the large quantities of oil in storage, Flagler and Rockefeller were able to promise the railroads a steady supply of oil for shipping. In return, the railroads billed the partnership at the regular rate and then secretly gave back some of the money they had charged. This payment was called a *kickback*.

Henry M. Flagler, the first of many energetic and talented executives hired by John D. Rockefeller, also became a good friend. "It was a friendship founded on business, which Mr. Flagler used to say was better than a business founded on friendship," Rockefeller wrote. "My experience leads me to agree with him."

Because of the advantages with the railroads that Rockefeller and Flagler had obtained for the partnership, the company flourished. They decided to incorporate their business, and the Standard Oil Company was born on January 10, 1870. Standard Oil was *capitalized*, or supplied with investment funds, of $1 million with Rockefeller as the principal shareholder. William Rockefeller, Flagler, Andrews, and two outside investors all received stock in the new corporation.

With his new company, Rockefeller made his move to buy out the other refineries in the Cleveland area. Smaller companies that were unable to compete with Rockefeller's rebate advantage with the railroad had no choice but to join Standard Oil or face ruin. By 1872, Rockefeller had succeeded in taking control of Cleveland's entire refining industry.

This was just the beginning. Rockefeller intended to take over the entire oil industry, never wavering from his belief that he was doing this for the industry's own good. But the producers and refiners in the Oil Region did not like Rockefeller's methods. They united and protested vigorously and publicly to the railroads, vowing not to sell their crude oil to the Standard Oil Company. By this time, however, Standard had grown so large that these threats meant nothing.

Using hidden companies and secret arrangements and deals, Rockefeller now moved to form a monopoly of the oil refineries. He sometimes used bribes, threats, and intimidation, not caring who he ruined on his way to attaining his goals. By 1880, Standard Oil refined 95 percent of the oil produced in the United States. In 1882, Rockefeller formed the Standard Oil Trust, a complex organization of 40 corporations that gave Standard Oil control of every aspect of the oil industry. Clearly, Rockefeller was well on his way to becoming the richest man in the United States.

With the offices of the trust established in New York, Rockefeller reluctantly moved his family from their quiet life in Cleveland to New York City. There they joined a local Baptist church and settled in a modest house, shunning New York society. The four Rockefeller children—Bessie, Alta, Edith, and John Davison Jr.—had no idea their father was a wealthy man. Rockefeller liked to think of himself as a country boy who lived simply, enjoying games and outings with his family. But at the office, he was an ironhanded tycoon who, like the group of powerful men he had worked with, became a millionaire from oil.

Even though Rockefeller tried to avoid publicity, the press began to depict him as greedy and power mad. Not bothered by this public outcry, Rockefeller instead focused his attention on threats to the oil industry. First, there was a concern that the oil supply in Pennsylvania would run out. When oil was discovered in Lima, Ohio, Rockefeller immediately bought up the supply.

Then overseas, the Standard monopoly was adversely affected by the development of the Baku oil fields in Russia, which began to supply Europe with oil in the late 1880s. Standard met this challenge by opening new markets in Asia, Africa, and South America.

When Edison invented the electric light bulb in 1879, it seemed that kerosene would eventually become unnecessary. But then the automobile appeared, creating an unquenchable thirst for oil and its by-products.

Now living on a large estate in Tarrytown, New York, John D. Rockefeller officially retired from Standard Oil in 1896. Nevertheless, his fortune continued to increase through the growth of Standard Oil stock and its dividends, making him America's first billionaire.

In 1902, *McClure's* magazine began a serialized account of the ruthless methods that had been used by the Standard Oil Company to centralize the oil industry. Written by Ida Tarbell, an investigative journalist, the series of articles ran for two years, capturing the public's interest and inciting its indignation. Rockefeller became the most hated man in America. Even the Baptist Church, which had always been a beneficiary of his generosity, questioned the advisability of accepting "tainted" money. Despised by a disapproving public, Rockefeller found solace with the family he cherished. He also began to develop ideas about what he could do with his money.

Investigative reporters like Ida Minerva Tarbell (1857-1944) were often called muckrakers—a *term from a character in John Bunyan's book* Pilgrim's Progress *who could only look down and spent all his time raking through the muck (which literally is mud and manure).*

*Swamped
with appeals
for money,
John D.
Rockefeller
hired Baptist
minister
Frederick T.
Gates to
advise him.*

Through the Baptist Church, Rockefeller had met a young preacher, Frederick T. Gates, whom he hired in 1891 to handle the huge quantity of charitable requests that came to Rockefeller daily. Gates investigated each appeal and gave Rockefeller recommendations for action. Gates quickly recognized that Rockefeller's fortune was rolling up "like an avalanche" and warned him to "distribute it faster than it grows. If you do not, it will crush you and your children, and your children's children."

Rockefeller agreed, but he wanted an organized and logical plan to follow. He believed that because God had given him the ability to make money, it was his duty to use his wealth for the good of humanity.

Giving money to charity had been a lifelong habit for Rockefeller and his wife. In fact, in 1884, Laura Rockefeller had encouraged her husband to give $5,000 to an Atlanta seminary for black women, which was later renamed Spelman College in honor of Laura's abolitionist parents. In 1887, Rockefeller gave $600,000 to revive another small seminary that had fallen on hard times. By 1910, Rockefeller had given more than $45 million to the highly respected school, now renamed the University of Chicago. Rockefeller referred to that donation as "the best investment I ever made."

Gates proposed that Rockefeller create a medical research facility in the United States, similar to the Pasteur Institute in Paris. The Rockefeller Institute for Medical Research was established in New York City in 1901 as the first U.S. laboratory with the stated purpose of finding cures for diseases. Its first head, Dr. Simon Flexner, developed a serum for treating meningitis. Another staff member, Dr. Alexis Carrel, pioneered the technique of blood transfusions. Now known as Rockefeller University, the institution continues to be one of the finest medical schools in the country.

In 1903, Rockefeller started the General Education Board (G.E.B.) to form joint programs with other philanthropies. (Andrew Carnegie was one of its trustees.) As its first project, the G.E.B. funded education of blacks

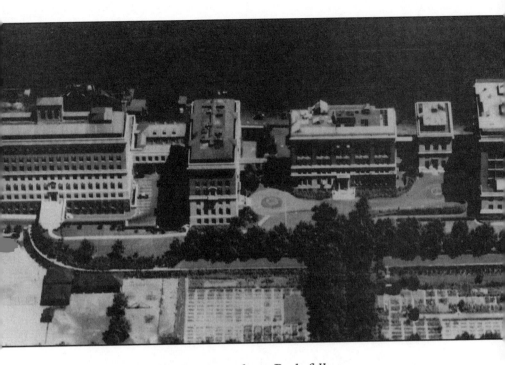

The Rockefeller Institute, later Rockefeller University, was built on a cliff overlooking the East River in New York City. The school continues to be an important research and medical center.

in the South. Later, it offered financial support to any U.S. medical school willing to use the recommendations of a Carnegie Foundation study to standardize its medical education. Schools such as Johns Hopkins, Yale, Harvard, Columbia, and the University of Chicago—medical schools that continue to enjoy a reputation for excellence—applied for these grants.

In 1909, Rockefeller set up the Rockefeller Sanitation Commission to send teams of doctors to the rural South to wipe out the scourge of hookworm, a common parasite in that region. Hookworms, which enter the human body when people walk barefoot on infected soil, can cause retardation and stunted growth in children. Some suspicious people thought the commission's efforts were just a scheme to make them buy shoes until they were shown, through microscopes, that hookworms actually did exist. Through its educational efforts, the Sanitation Commission ultimately wiped out hookworm in 52 countries around the world.

Four years later, in 1913, Rockefeller established the Rockefeller Foundation. Funded with nearly $200 million, it was to be administered by professionals who would understand its commitment "to promote the well-being of mankind throughout the world." In the years since it was organized, the Rockefeller Foundation has granted millions of dollars for research in medicine, public health, social sciences, the humanities, and agriculture, as well as scholarships and fellowships, and it continues to distribute funds to support programs in these areas. In 1994, the foundation gave $1 million to the World Health Organization.

New efforts by the foundation include support of projects focused on population science, the environment, and human rights. In the mid-1990s, the foundation had assets of almost $2.5 billion, making it the eighth largest foundation in the United States. Annual distributions by the foundation during that time exceeded $93 million.

John D. Rockefeller gives a young boy a dime on his way into the First Baptist Church in 1929, a gesture he repeated often in his later years.

During Rockefeller's last decades, the activities of his foundation caused the public to view him in a positive light. While Rockefeller did not give his money away to achieve public favor, he took pride in the many ways his philanthropy improved people's lives.

John D. Rockefeller died on May 23, 1937, just six weeks before his ninety-eighth birthday. His family had always been paramount in his life, and he taught his children and grandchildren the values of responsible

John D. Rockefeller Jr. (1874-1960) carried on his father's tradition of giving. He restored Colonial Williamsburg in Virginia and donated the site on which the United Nations headquarters was built in New York. His wife, Abby Aldrich Rockefeller, helped to found the Museum of Modern Art and gave the organization most of her large art collection.

Nelson Aldrich Rockefeller (1908-1979), grandson of John D. Rockefeller, served as governor of New York from 1959 to 1973. After Gerald Ford attained the presidency upon Richard Nixon's resignation, Rockefeller was named vice-president of the United States in 1974, a post he filled until 1977.

money management—to always save a portion and give a portion. Having passed this legacy and the mantle of responsibility to his children and grandchildren, he assured that the Rockefeller dynasty would continue in its work for the public good. His son, John D. Rockefeller Jr., and his grandsons, Nelson, Laurance, Winthrop, David, and John D. Rockefeller III, have all given of themselves and their wealth to improve society.

*Successful retailer Julius Rosenwald (1862-1932)
used his wealth to help educate African Americans
and to fight racial prejudice.*

5

Julius Rosenwald
Giving for Today

*A*mong philanthropists, the name of Julius Rosenwald
is almost forgotten. But that is exactly what he wanted.
He left no endowment or prize. His name is not embla-
zoned on any building or letterhead. There is no existing
foundation named for him. Yet along with Andrew
Carnegie and John D. Rockefeller, historians rank Julius
Rosenwald as one of the world's great philanthropists.

While Rosenwald's benefactions during his lifetime
exceeded $63 million, it was his ideas that had the most
impact on contemporary philanthropy. He strongly

believed that donated money should be used in the generation in which it was made. He also believed that philanthropic enterprises should come to a close at the end of the donor's life or, at most, a single generation after the donor's death. "The generation which has contributed to the making of a millionaire," he said, "should also be the one to profit by his generosity."

Julius's parents, Samuel and Augusta Rosenwald, were German Jewish immigrants who met and married shortly after arriving in the United States. They settled in Springfield, Illinois, where Samuel took over a clothing store from his wife's brothers when they left to start another business in New York.

Growing up in Springfield, where he was born on August 12, 1862, Julius Rosenwald never thought about becoming a rich man. Instead, he expected to work in the clothing business like his father. Julius enjoyed helping in his father's store, selling customers the paper collars that most men wore in those days.

Along with his three brothers and two sisters, Julius attended public school and did odd jobs on weekends when he was not needed in his father's store. In 1879, after two years of high school, Julius went to New York to serve an apprenticeship with his uncles, who had become leading clothing manufacturers. His salary as an apprentice was $5 a week.

Five years later, after Julius finished his apprenticeship, he and his brother Morris, who had joined him in

New York, decided to open their own clothing business. Struggling against stiff competition, they became discouraged with New York City. Rosenwald decided there would be more opportunities manufacturing men's summer clothing in the booming midwestern city of Chicago. With their fathers' financial help, Rosenwald, his brother, and a cousin, Julius E. Weil, opened the firm of Rosenwald & Weil.

In 1890, Rosenwald married Augusta Nusbaum, a young woman who had also come to Chicago from New York when her father entered the clothing business. From the start, their interests were the same and, as the years went by, Augusta strongly encouraged her husband in his philanthropic endeavors.

While Rosenwald was building his clothing business in Chicago, two young men named Richard Sears and Alvah Roebuck began selling watches through a mail-order catalog. After a successful year together, they named their partnership Sears, Roebuck and Company. In addition to watches, they added clothing, sporting goods, carriages, harnesses, and other general merchandise to their catalog. Through hard work and long hours, Sears and Roebuck tripled their sales in three years. But the demands of the work took its toll on Roebuck's health. In 1895, he handed over his stock in the business to Richard Sears and asked him to sell it.

Through his brother-in-law, Aaron Nusbaum, Rosenwald learned of the opportunity to buy into Sears,

Roebuck and Company. For an investment of $37,500, he bought a one-quarter interest in the company and gained an exciting new challenge. (Nusbaum bought the other one-quarter interest, which Rosenwald later purchased from him.) Rosenwald ended his association with the clothing business to become an active partner in the growing mail-order operation.

With Sears as president and Rosenwald as vice-president, the new partners made a good team. Sears's

By 1996, the company founded by Richard Warren Sears (1863-1914) operated 820 stores that posted sales of about $38 billion.

strength was in creative advertising, while Rosenwald excelled in merchandising, financial management, and sound business judgment.

Before Rosenwald joined the company, Sears had brought in a large number of orders by developing an attractive 500-page mail-order catalog. But Rosenwald found the plant where the orders were processed to be disorganized and inefficient. To serve their customers better, Rosenwald reorganized the warehouse so the large volume of orders could be quickly and accurately filled. Rosenwald personally stood behind the quality and performance of the company's goods by offering customers the innovative promise "Your money back if not satisfied." This unconditional, money-back guarantee became the cornerstone of the integrity of Sears, Roebuck and Company.

With a rural population spread over the country, often far from towns and stores, the mail-order business grew rapidly. By 1898, the Sears catalog contained over 1,200 pages. Customers eagerly awaited the catalog's arrival in the mail, poring over its pages to make their selections. People often arranged catalog-reading parties, gathering in groups to look at and discuss the many items featured in the Sears, Roebuck and Company catalog. One customer even sent a check with instructions for the company to choose her wedding gown and trousseau!

Because the catalogs contained written descriptions alongside pictures of the merchandise, teachers in rural

The cover of the 1899 Sears, Roebuck and Company's
catalog promised a cornucopia of goods at low prices.

schools often used the catalogs as textbooks to improve reading. Today, these early Sears catalogs have historical value as a chronicle of the changes in national tastes, customs, and prices throughout the twentieth century.

With Rosenwald's capable management and Sears's ingenious advertising ability, the business mushroomed from 475 employees in 1897 to more than 10,000 in 1914. During that same period, sales increased from $3 million to more than $100 million, giving Sears, Roebuck and Company an edge over Montgomery Ward, its greatest competitor.

By 1904, the company needed a larger and more modern facility to handle its huge volume of sales. In order to raise the millions necessary for construction, Sears and Rosenwald went to a New York investment banking firm to borrow the money. Instead of giving them a loan, the firm's senior officer advised the two partners to make their business a public company. To accomplish this, two of the largest brokerage houses in New York City underwrote and issued shares of stock in Sears, Roebuck and Company to be sold to the public. The stock offering provided the company with $40 million to finance its new building.

Confident that the value of Sears stock would increase, Rosenwald wanted to share his good fortune with others. He offered friends, relatives, and employees an opportunity to purchase shares, even advancing them money if they needed it. Rosenwald's confidence proved

The large, efficient headquarters that helped Sears, Roebuck and Company become so successful is shown here in 1925.

to be well-founded—one share of Sears, Roebuck and Company stock purchased in 1906 for $50 had increased in value to $2,820 by 1928.

With money from the sale of their stock, Rosenwald planned and supervised the construction of the company's new plant. Costing over $5 million, with 3 million square feet of floor space, the building complex was ready for occupancy in 1906. It was the largest place of business in the world, designed to be one enormous distribution center. Rosenwald took great pride in showing visitors around the efficient new headquarters, where orders were filled on the day they came in and sent on their way to customers by nightfall.

In 1909, after Sears retired because of poor health, Rosenwald became president of Sears, Roebuck and Company. As its new president, Rosenwald began a program of changes. To ensure customer satisfaction, he revised the catalog copy to describe the exact contents of the products more accurately. He offered stock options to his executives, and he developed for all of his employees one of the best profit-sharing systems ever inaugurated in the United States.

Rosenwald brought his eldest son, Lessing, into the business in 1911. Rosenwald told his son he would receive no special favors and let him know that any advancement would depend entirely on his own merits. Lessing Rosenwald rose through the executive ranks to succeed his father as chairman of the board in 1932.

Between 1900 and 1914, Rosenwald's personal fortune increased rapidly. While he never felt he needed to apologize for anything he had done to acquire his wealth, he once remarked to a friend, "I really feel ashamed to have so much money." He, therefore, felt a strong obligation to use his wealth for the benefit of humanity.

Raised in the Jewish tradition that taught charity as an obligation, Rosenwald found a kindred soul in his wife, Augusta. Early in their marriage, he once gave away $2,500, a sum much larger than he could afford at the time. He worried about telling his young bride about his impetuous decision, but when he did, she set his mind at ease by telling him, "Don't ever hesitate, Jule, to give money. I will never stand in the way of any gift you want to make."

Rosenwald's first serious philanthropic interest centered on the work of the Associated Jewish Charities of Chicago. He became the organization's president in 1907 and for the rest of his life remained its largest contributor.

During this time, Julius Rosenwald developed his philanthropic philosophy of giving away money without any restrictions. He firmly believed that directors and trustees should have the discretion to use the principal of an endowment, as well as the earned interest. In an article for *Atlantic Monthly*, Rosenwald wrote, "Perpetuities for specific objectives are a mistake because times change and with them need and circumstances change. The dead hand has been proved to be a hindrance to the progress of mankind."

Rosenwald asserted that ideas, not money, were the real endowments. He believed that private philanthropy should initiate novel or unpopular projects and then, after their value had been proved, encourage government to give them permanent support. He backed up his belief by persuading others to give as generously to worthy causes as he did. Soliciting funds for charity was one of his favorite activities.

In 1917, Rosenwald established the Julius Rosenwald Fund to work toward the "well-being of mankind." Self-liquidating, the foundation was legally bound to spend interest and principal within 25 years. Always concerned with the problems of the deprived, Rosenwald pledged $6 million to help settle Russian Jews in agricultural colonies following World War I. In 1920, he gave $100,000 to feed children in Germany.

But the people Rosenwald felt the greatest concern for were African Americans who lacked equality in education. As a Jew whose people had endured discrimination, he felt he could not allow other groups to suffer from prejudice and persecution. And as an American citizen who cherished the ideals of democracy, Rosenwald believed his country could not go forward if a large segment of its population was left behind.

Rosenwald was greatly influenced by Booker T. Washington's book, *Up from Slavery*. Like Washington, who founded the black vocational school Tuskegee Institute, Rosenwald believed that education and the skills to acquire good jobs were the greatest needs in the black community.

In the early 1900s, 80 percent of American blacks still lived in the South, and most of them were employed in agriculture or as unskilled laborers. Few black children had the opportunity to go to school. In Alabama at that time, about 20 percent of black children were enrolled in school, compared to 60 percent of white children, and the average school term for southern black children was four months, compared to seven months for white students.

To correct these inequalities, Rosenwald helped to establish more than 5,300 schools for blacks in rural areas

Booker T. Washington (1856-1915) and Julius Rosenwald met in 1911 and became good friends. Rosenwald's gifts and fundraising on behalf of the Tuskegee Institute gave Washington more time to run his school. Rosenwald was elected a trustee at Tuskegee in 1912, a post he held for the rest of his life.

of 15 southern states and to pay the teachers' salaries. In order to improve the qualifications of black teachers, Rosenwald also funded schools for higher education where black teachers received their training. The total cost for these Rosenwald schools, built between 1913 and 1932, was $28 million. Rosenwald contributed the first $4.3 million in "seed" money.

In his practice of offering "seed" money, often referred to as challenge grants, Rosenwald showed as much enterprise and vision in bestowing his wealth as he had in accumulating it. These initial gifts were meant to stimulate gifts from others and to be productive social investments. The black communities where Rosenwald funded schoolhouses in the South met his challenge grants and raised $4.7 million. Public authorities funded the remaining cost of the schools with tax dollars.

Rosenwald used the same strategy to fund YMCAs in black communities. He pledged $25,000 to every community that raised $75,000 towards the construction of a YMCA. This offer triggered nationwide fundraising and resulted in 24 new YMCA buildings. Today, challenge grants are a common and effective approach used by fundraisers.

As a leading citizen of Chicago, Rosenwald possessed a sense of civic responsibility, a feeling that he owed time and money to improving the community in which he had prospered. His home was a meeting place for discussion among the city's leaders. As a trustee of the University of Chicago, his gifts over the years totaled more than $6 million.

In 1926, with more than $6 million in donations, Rosenwald helped to establish the Museum of Science and Industry in Chicago. It was initially known as the "Rosenwald Industrial Museum," but Rosenwald steadfastly refused to have his name attached permanently to institutions that had received his contributions and insisted the name be changed to the Museum of Science

The construction of the Museum of Science and Industry, funded by Julius Rosenwald, was near completion when this photograph was taken in November 1930.

and Industry. A generation of Chicagoans, however, persisted in calling the building the "Rosenwald Museum."

A modest man, Rosenwald once said, "No one was more surprised at my sudden landing in the midst of America's multimillionaire class than I was myself." He also believed that "most large fortunes are made by men of mediocre ability who tumbled into a lucky opportunity and could not help but get rich."

In his lifetime, Rosenwald gave away more than $63 million of his own wealth. But through his influence, many more millions of dollars were raised for causes he promoted, with millions of people benefiting either directly or indirectly from his generosity.

Julius Rosenwald, who considered philanthropy to be his duty, told his doctor before he died on January 6, 1932, that he regretted he had not been able to do more. He firmly believed that "unselfish effort and helpfulness to others ennobles life, not because of what it does for others but more because of what it does for ourselves."

Julius Rosenwald with his family at their estate in Ravinia, Illinois, which they purchased in 1911. His wife, Augusta, holds their grandson, Armand Deutsch Jr., son of their daughter, Adele Rosenwald Deutsch (right). The Rosenwald home was often filled with family and friends, especially on Sundays.

George Eastman (1854-1932) not only invented new ways to take photographs, but he also used innovative business methods to market his products worldwide.

6

George Eastman
The Click Heard 'Round the World

*I*nventors are creative pioneers who usually display characteristics of curiosity, ingenuity, and patience. Sometimes inventors develop ideas to solve problems in the workplace or to improve people's daily lives.

George Eastman, the man who pioneered the film industry and made Kodak a household word, began with only one goal—to make a new hobby easy and enjoyable for himself. A modest, shy man, Eastman developed his hobby into an industry that brought the joys of photography and motion pictures to millions of people around the world. Then, as his wealth accumulated, he became a great philanthropist with a profound desire to distribute his money where it would do the most good.

George Eastman was born on July 12, 1854, in Waterville, New York, the youngest of three children. When George was six years old, he moved with his parents and two older sisters to Rochester, New York. There his father, George Washington Eastman, established a small business college.

Two years later, George's father died, leaving the family with very little money. George's mother, Maria Kilbourn Eastman, struggled to provide for the family by taking in boarders. Eight-year-old George tried to fill his father's shoes by earning money from small jobs.

At the age of 13, George left school to accept his first steady job as a messenger in an insurance office for $3 a week. His salary increased to $35 a month when he advanced to a better position in the office. After several years, he left the insurance company to become a junior bookkeeper at the Rochester Savings Bank. By the time George was 20 years old, his earnings amounted to $1,000 annually. That salary enabled him to relieve his mother of the financial responsibilities for their home.

George grew up with a sense of adventure and curiosity, always wanting to try something new and to travel. While he was planning a trip to Santo Domingo (now a city in the Dominican Republic), one of his associates suggested he take along a camera to record his activities. Although he never took the vacation, Eastman bought the photographic equipment and soon became thoroughly engrossed in photography as a hobby.

Photography in 1878 involved working with about 50 pounds of equipment. The only camera available was large and heavy and required a tripod to hold it steady. There was no such thing as film, only photographic plates, which were squares of glass coated with a gluey

When George Eastman began taking pictures, his equipment looked like this large camera, complete with tripod. Inside the tent are glass photographic plates and the chemicals used to develop them.

chemical solution called collodion. A bath in silver nitrate made the plates sensitive to light. While a plate was wet, the photographer put it into the camera, took the picture, and then developed it on the spot. Outdoor hobbyists, like Eastman, had to carry their darkroom with them.

Although Eastman loved photography, he disliked carrying the cumbersome equipment. So he began to search for a simpler way to take pictures that would eliminate the heavy wet plates, which often leaked. In 1878, he read about Charles Bennett (1840-1927) in the *British Journal of Photography*. Bennett had discovered a method of heating a different type of plate coating, called a gelatin emulsion, to produce a dry photographic plate. After experimenting in his mother's kitchen, Eastman came up with his own formula for producing a dry plate. To avoid coating the plates by hand, he also invented and patented a machine with a rubber roller that evenly applied the gelatin emulsion to the plate.

"At first," Eastman later recalled, "I wanted to make photography simpler merely for my own convenience, but soon I thought of the possibilities of commercial production." He became completely absorbed in this idea, sometimes working all night and catching up on sleep on the weekends. Finally, he decided to leave his job at the bank to go into business producing dry plates.

In 1881, Eastman formed a partnership with one of his mother's former boarders, Henry Alvah Strong. Interested in Eastman's experiments, Strong provided the

Henry Alvah Strong (1838-1919) owned a company that manufactured buggy whips at the time he became George Eastman's business partner.

financial backing needed to start the Eastman Dry Plate Company. As well as an active business partner, he also became one of Eastman's closest friends and advisors.

Orders poured in after Eastman advertised his new dry plate in a number of photography journals. Soon the company was turning out 4,000 plates a month. Success seemed certain until, in February 1882, wholesalers began complaining of plates that went "dead." They could no longer produce photographic images.

To deal with this product failure, Eastman first assured all of his unhappy customers that the Eastman Dry Plate Company would supply them with good plates. Next, Eastman performed almost 500 experiments to determine why the plates had gone bad. Finally, he discovered the problem—a supplier of one of the ingredients in the gelatin emulsion had changed the formula without telling Eastman about the change. From this experience, Eastman learned an important lesson—to test every product coming into the factory before using it.

Even though the dry plate business became quite profitable, Eastman continued to experiment because he wanted to develop something to replace the heavy glass plate. After countless experiments with numerous materials and chemicals, Eastman came up with strips of paper coated with collodion and a sensitized gelatin emulsion. After being exposed and developed, the paper could be separated from the negative image and a print made from the image. Eastman had invented transparent film. This lightweight, flexible product would completely change the photography industry and make its inventor a millionaire.

In 1884, Eastman hired William H. Walker, a former camera manufacturer, and together they worked on the problem of inventing something to hold the new film in the camera. First, they made a lightweight wood frame that could be affixed to the back of any standard camera. Then they produced a roll of film by winding a measured length of film around a spool. This handy, 24-exposure roll could be attached to the roll holder and turned with a clock key located on the outside of the camera.

By 1885, the new paper-backed film was available for shipment. But it didn't catch on as Eastman had expected. Portrait photographers preferred the old way of working under a hood, changing plates while keeping their subjects mesmerized in a studio. While outdoor photographers liked the convenience of the new film, there were too few of them to sustain a business. Photography was still too expensive and complicated to be a practical hobby.

In 1888, after working for three more years with Walker, who was now one of his partners, Eastman produced a simple box camera. Although clumsy by today's standards, its 22-ounce weight was a vast improvement over the old, heavier cameras.

Eastman's box camera contained film for 100 photos. After taking the pictures, the amateur photographer mailed the exposed film, still in the camera, to the Eastman Company for developing and printing. Because the new film had to be loaded in complete darkness, the company would reload the camera with new film and send it back for the customer's next series of photographs.

Eastman needed a name for his new camera. He wanted a strong word that was easy to remember and one that everyone would associate with his camera. The name had to comply with foreign trademark laws. Moreover, Eastman also wanted to be sure that the name was not likely to be misspelled.

After much pondering, Eastman decided to use "K," a sound that is pronounced the same in every language, as the first and last letters of his camera's name. He then tried different combinations of letters until he came up with the word "Kodak." The name was short, it could not be mispronounced, and Eastman thought it was "euphonious and snappy"—like the shutter click of a camera. Kodak became a word synonymous with camera, known the world over.

Eastman first advertised his small, easy-to-use camera with the slogan, "You press the button—we do the rest." Taking quick pictures, or snapshots, caught on as Eastman's Kodak camera revolutionized the world of photography. By 1889, his company was worth $1 million, and in December Eastman incorporated the company. Three years later, he changed the name to the Eastman Kodak Company.

In 1889, Eastman received a letter from Thomas A. Edison, ordering a Kodak camera. Having already invented the electric light bulb and the phonograph, Edison was then working on a motion-picture camera. A working relationship developed between the two inventors, and by 1891 Eastman produced the film suitable for the first motion-picture camera, Edison's Kinetoscope. Eastman Kodak Company became the first to manufacture and market film in *reels*, or continuous strips. Interestingly, the two men who worked together by mail and telephone did not meet in person until 1907.

As Eastman's business increased rapidly both in the United States and abroad, the company needed larger and more modern manufacturing and research facilities. In 1890, Eastman purchased a large tract of land near Rochester, New York, and built Kodak Park.

In 1891, Eastman Kodak introduced prewound spooled film, which allowed users to load their cameras in the daylight instead of having to send them back to the company for reloading. This improvement increased

George Eastman in 1890, aiming his own Kodak camera while bound for Europe aboard the mail steamer Galia

sales further. By 1896, Eastman produced his 100,000th camera, and the amount of film and photographic paper manufactured each month by his company could be measured in hundreds of miles.

As manufacturing techniques improved, Eastman was able to mass produce smaller, cheaper cameras. He marketed the Bulls-Eye camera for $12, followed by the Falcon for $5. Finally, the Brownie was introduced to the world in 1900 to sell for just $1.

Although Eastman had developed the Brownie to appeal to children, adults also loved it and bought the camera for themselves as well as for their children and grandchildren. The Brownie soon became the most popular camera of all. George Eastman had simplified photography and made it available to people of all ages.

Because Eastman wanted his company to be the leader in the photographic industry, he hired the best scientific minds from leading universities to work on new and improved products. He once said, "To rest content with results achieved is the first sign of decay."

Eastman also cared deeply about the welfare of his employees, so he instituted a number of benefits that were unprecedented in American industry at the time. Pension plans, bonus incentives, accident-reduction measures, and health care were some of the advantages received by the employees of the Eastman Kodak Company. His personnel practices, too, were ahead of the time. He hired several women chemists and his secretary,

The Brownie camera, introduced in 1900 and priced at $1, became the most popular of all the Kodak cameras. (A brownie is a sprite, or tiny man, believed to do helpful work at night.)

Alice Whitney, was an important figure in the company. He also employed ex-convicts and people with disabilities.

One of Eastman's innovative ideas was a "Suggestion Scheme." He offered employees cash rewards for practical suggestions about how to improve manufacturing, building construction, and safety. Over a period of several years, the company adopted many of the hundreds of ideas suggested by Eastman employees. In fact, through their cooperation, the number of accidents decreased so dramatically that, in 1913, the company held the record for accident prevention among all the manufacturing companies in the United States.

As his wealth increased, Eastman made the decision to give his money away while he could control how it would be used. "If you leave it by will," he said, "five years may pass, and the scheme you devised may be unfitting to the new circumstances. The executors may be so hampered by the conditions of the will that successful use of the funds is difficult. It is more fun to give money away than to will it. And that is why I give."

In 1917, Eastman launched his philanthropy by establishing dental clinics in Rochester, New York, that provided free treatment for children and adults. During the last half of the nineteenth century, dentistry had become a more exact science, but children's teeth were often neglected. Eastman believed that "money spent in the care of children's teeth is one of the wisest expenditures that can be made."

Eastman's interest in preventive dentistry and oral surgery inspired him to establish dental clinics not only in the United States, but also in the European cities where Eastman Kodak Company had factories—London, Paris, Stockholm, Brussels, and Rome.

Being a private person, Eastman tried to avoid attention in his philanthropy. In 1912, for example, the Massachusetts Institute of Technology (M.I.T.) sought Eastman's financial help for a new campus in Cambridge. Wanting to support the school where many of his chemists received their training, Eastman pledged $3 million as an anonymous donor, "Mr. Smith." Speculation ran wild as to the identity of the mysterious Mr. Smith who was giving away millions, but no one came close to guessing the donor's identity.

When a representative of the university called on Eastman to solicit money for a new chemistry building, the ruse continued. Not wanting to reveal his identity as Mr. Smith, Eastman listened patiently to the explanation of the building fund. When his visitor asked him for a gift of $300,000, Eastman wrote out a check for the requested amount. How Eastman must have enjoyed himself as his grateful caller, unaware the check was written by the generous "Mr. Smith," thanked him profusely.

In 1920, after eight years of suspense and a total of $11 million in gifts to M.I.T. (plus the $300,000 given under his own name), Eastman finally allowed his identity to be revealed. According to the press coverage, when the announcement was made at an alumni association dinner, it raised "a bedlam of cheering" among the 1,100 men and women in attendance.

Eastman's gifts, eventually reaching more than $100 million, were spread out among many worthy organizations, both in Rochester and around the world. More than half of his fortune went to universities such as M.I.T. and the University of Rochester, and to black colleges, including the Tuskegee Institute. The University of Rochester received the largest gift, over $35 million, which established the Eastman School of Music as well as a school of medicine and dentistry.

George Eastman loved music and flowers and surrounded himself with both. This photograph shows the conservatory of his mansion set for a breakfast in 1919. Behind the flowers is an organ, which a musician began to play when Eastman entered the room. His home and gardens have been restored as a museum.

During the time Eastman enjoyed giving his money away, he indulged himself as well. On a 12-acre parcel of land in Rochester, Eastman, who never married, built a mansion with extensive gardens for himself and his mother. Eastman also realized his dreams of travel, going to Africa on safari in 1926 with famed wildlife researchers and photographers Martin and Osa Johnson.

After returning from his second trip to Africa in 1928, Eastman became ill with a painful and progressive spinal disease. Walking became difficult, and doctors told him his condition was incurable. Eastman could not face the prospect of becoming an invalid. In a note to friends, he wrote, "My work is done. Why wait?" The man who brought the joys and wonders of photography to the world killed himself on March 14, 1932.

Perhaps as much as any other single invention, photographic film has touched the lives of almost every person in the world. George Eastman's inventions are the basis for a great portion of today's mass entertainment. In education and in many of the arts, film provides a medium for understanding and enlightenment. And with film indispensable in medical and dental diagnosis, it is often the key to scientific research. But it was George Eastman's philanthropy, which provided for education in research, medical and dental health, as well as enrichment in the arts, that has given the world an even greater and continuing legacy.

Will Keith Kellogg (1860-1951) changed the breakfast habits of many people when he began manufacturing and selling corn flakes in 1906. His fortune established a foundation dedicated to helping people help themselves.

7

Will Keith Kellogg
The Corn Flake King

*I*t's hard to imagine a time when there was no such thing as ready-to-eat breakfast cereal. Before the twentieth century, people either ate hot cooked cereals such as oatmeal or eggs with meat, fried potatoes, or biscuits. Cold, ready-to-eat breakfast cereal was introduced to the public by Will Keith Kellogg, a man who so revolutionized the way people ate breakfast that he became known as "The Corn Flake King."

Will Kellogg, a shy introvert who seldom smiled or laughed in public, lived his adult life in three separate phases. He spent his early adult years quietly working for his domineering older brother. In midlife, Kellogg entered the business world, emerging as an energetic merchandising genius who built a highly profitable breakfast cereal company. In the last phase of his long life, he worked for the advancement of human welfare by using his wealth to establish a foundation dedicated to helping others to help themselves.

On April 7, 1860, Will Keith Kellogg was born to John Preston Kellogg and his second wife, Ann Janette, in Battle Creek, Michigan. His parents were devout Seventh-Day Adventists, a group of Christians whose faith centers on the *advent*, or second coming, of Christ. Adventists also observe the Sabbath on Saturday and practice a simple way of life that includes abstinence from tobacco, alcohol, coffee, tea, and meat.

The Kelloggs raised their 14 children in this strict atmosphere and expected them to work long and hard. Yet they were generous people who often helped their neighbors. In 1850, John Kellogg became involved in the underground railroad, sheltering runaway black slaves on their way to freedom in Canada.

Will's formal education ended at age 13 when he started working as an apprentice in his father's broom factory. By the time he was 14, he was on the road selling brooms and enjoying the freedom of traveling throughout Michigan by train. Once, while his father was laid up with a broken hip, Will took over the responsibility of running

Will Kellogg on his fifteenth birthday, posing with the brooms he sold

the factory. But looking back on his brief childhood later in life, Kellogg once reflected, "As a boy I never learned to play."

Deciding that he needed additional education, Will enrolled in a bookkeeping course in nearby Kalamazoo. Anxious to return to Battle Creek to see Ella Davis, his "best girl," he worked hard to complete the one-year course in just three months. Having a skill to make a living gave Will the confidence he needed to ask Ella to be his bride. Will and Ella Osborn Davis were married on November 3, 1880.

Soon Kellogg, a married man with responsibilities, went to work for his brother, Dr. John Harvey Kellogg. Older than Will by eight years, John Harvey was a physician and a prominent advocate of health reform. He operated a successful sanitarium in Battle Creek, based on the Seventh-Day Adventist beliefs in proper rest and exercise, water treatments, vegetarian food, and abstinence from alcohol, tobacco, and caffeine.

The forerunner of the modern health spas so popular today, the "San," as it was known, used natural methods to restore health without the use of drugs. Because of John Harvey's brilliant, flamboyant, and enthusiastic personality, people from all walks of life flocked to the San for rejuvenation.

A business manager without the title, Will kept the San running smoothly and worked long hours with very little compensation. He started at the meager salary of $9 per week, and three years passed before his brother gave him a weekly raise of $1! Will often left for work in the morning before his children were awake and returned home after they were in bed.

For Will, the hardest part of the job was interviewing people who needed medical help but did not have the funds to pay for it. The San had to limit the number

Dr. John Harvey Kellogg's charismatic personality attracted patients to his health spa known as the "San."

of free cases it accepted. Will often made special appeals to his brother or to the board or even paid for a patient's care himself. He hoped that one day he would be in a position to help more people.

The success of the San was due to the talents of both brothers, who were as different as night and day. John, the innovative genius with a showman's flair, cared for his patients while Will, using his organizational and bookkeeping skills, kept the institution financially sound.

But Will, totally dominated by his brother, led a grim, thankless existence. In 1884, he wrote in his diary, "I am afraid that I will always be a poor man the way things look now." Then things began to change—dramatically.

Will often assisted his brother in the San's experimental kitchen, where they developed and tested new health foods for their clients. The patients of the San liked the new products so much that they often asked to purchase them to take home. These sales convinced the doctor to go into the food business. John established the Sanitas Food Company in 1893 and put Will in charge. Instead of giving his younger brother an increase in salary, the doctor promised Will one-fourth of any profits from the new company. Thus challenged to add to his income, Will worked hard to build the company into a substantial enterprise by developing new foods.

One of the foods the doctor wanted for his new company was a more digestible substitute for bread. Turning the problem over to Will, the doctor told him to boil wheat to break it down and then figure out a way to flake it to make it easy to eat.

Boiling the wheat resulted in an unsatisfactory, gummy mixture. Will decided to spread it on a set of grinding rollers. After a lucky interruption, during which time the cooked wheat changed into a more workable consistency, he rolled out one individual wheat flake from each wheat grain. The flakes were tough and rather tasteless until they were toasted in the oven. When the finished wheat flakes were introduced, they became a great favorite of the San patients.

Not satisfied with his new product, Will continued to experiment to improve his flaked cereal. He decided to use corn instead of wheat; then he added sugar and salt and toasted the flakes. He ended up with an especially tasty product—corn flakes.

As other health foods developed by the Sanitas Food Company evolved into breakfast foods, Will recognized the possibilities for profit in selling them nationwide—not just as health foods, but as something good to eat. He especially wanted to promote his promising corn flake product, but the doctor rejected Will's idea. John feared any such promotional effort would jeopardize his medical reputation as well as the prestige of the sanitarium.

Cereal businesses by the dozen in the Battle Creek area were already trying to capitalize on the brothers' invention and the San's reputation. Most of them failed. One entrepreneur who succeeded was C. W. Post, a former patient, who opened a successful cereal factory a few miles away from the sanitarium.

Finally, Will made the decision to go into business for himself. He was preparing to leave in 1902 when a great fire burned the wood sanitarium to the ground. With a strong sense of duty, Will Keith postponed his departure by four years until the San was rebuilt.

In 1906, Kellogg purchased the right to make corn flakes from his brother. Instead of cash, Will paid John with shares of stock in his new company—the Battle Creek Toasted Corn Flake Company. (In 1925, Will changed the name to the Kellogg Company.) Even though skeptics called his product "horse food," Kellogg knew that consistent quality and the Kellogg name would make his product stand out among its competitors.

Surprisingly, the shy, quiet Kellogg displayed an amazing talent for marketing, capturing the imagination of the American homemaker. To get his infant company off the ground, Kellogg launched an intensive, bold, and imaginative advertising campaign using magazines, newspapers, and billboards. Spending a large amount of money on advertising was risky, but Kellogg was determined to convince the public that his corn flakes were "The Original and Best."

Now Kellogg had to solve another problem—how to persuade grocers to stock his product. Kellogg met this challenge by placing an ad in *The Ladies' Home Journal* magazine. In the form of a letter, the ad acknowledged, "This announcement violates all the rules of good advertising." It then proceeded to invite the magazine's readers to pressure their grocers to stock corn flakes. For doing this, they could use the coupon supplied at the bottom of the letter to get a three months' supply of corn flakes—free! In effect, it made housewives—the readers of the magazine—willing saleswomen for Kellogg's company. His ad proved to be one of the most brilliant advertising ideas ever used.

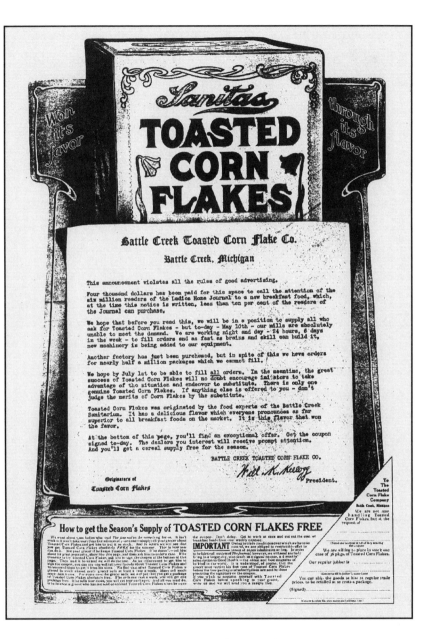

This advertisement appearing in the July 1906 issue of The Ladies' Home Journal *broke "all the rules of good advertising"—and sold a lot of corn flakes.*

During his first year in business, Kellogg gave away over 4 million samples, certain that once people tried corn flakes, they would continue to buy them. His intuition proved correct as millions of people began to buy and serve *Kellogg's Corn Flakes®* for breakfast.

There were more than 40 copycat companies in Battle Creek trying to take advantage of the ready-to-eat cereal craze. Kellogg thought of a clever way to end any confusion for buyers about which product was his. He put his signature, *W. K. Kellogg*, on every carton of his cereal with the slogan, *"The Original Has This Signature."®* Soon sales of Kellogg's cereal surpassed the competition, and W. K. Kellogg was crowned "the Corn Flake King."

Kellogg drove himself and his staff with tremendous energy. He personally handled all the problems of organizing, financing, and increasing the production capacity of his company. Hoping to establish a line of succession, Kellogg brought one of his two sons, John Leonard, into his growing business in 1908.

With the same drive and energy as his father, John made numerous inventive contributions to the Kellogg Company, such as new food products and improvements in protective packaging. Unfortunately, conflicts and disagreements between father and son resulted in John's forced resignation in 1925 after a 17-year association with the company.

Once again, Kellogg tried for a family successor by grooming John's son and his favorite grandson, John

John L. Kellogg (1883-1950) photographed in 1908, the year he joined his father's growing cereal business

Leonard Kellogg Jr., to come into the business. But because of physical and emotional problems, the young man was unable to handle the pressures and responsibilities that his grandfather heaped upon him. Leaving the company in 1937, John Jr. later committed suicide after another business failure.

With Kellogg's hope for a family dynasty shattered, he directed his energies toward another dream—helping others. After his banker had told him he was a million-aire, Kellogg recalled the sad plight of the many needy patients he had interviewed while working at the San and how he had wished he could have helped more of them. Now he could.

During the 1920s and 1930s, Kellogg personally helped family and friends with funds for emergencies, such as school, health, or funeral expenses. At his business, he assisted his female employees by installing a nursery that included a medical and dental clinic. Kellogg created the 25-Year Club to honor veteran employees, and he also contributed a block of company stock to fund a separate 25-Year Trust that made emergency benefits available to its members.

In 1925, Kellogg decided to establish a more sys-tematic way to distribute his donations. With a board of directors, he formed the Fellowship Corporation. Over the next five years, the agency distributed almost $1 mil-lion to fund projects, such as an agriculture school, a bird sanctuary, and schools and child-care facilities around the community of Battle Creek.

Remembering his own unhappy childhood, Kellogg especially enjoyed improving children's lives with projects such as the construction of schools, camps, and play-grounds. Because he "got a kick" out of giving his money away, he never thought of himself as a philanthropist.

Soon after the Fellowship Corporation began functioning, Kellogg saw that he would need a stronger organization with full-time trustees and a professional staff. As his fortune grew, he said, "It has been much easier to make money than to know how to spend it wisely." In 1930, Kellogg launched the W. K. Kellogg Foundation.

Over the next 21 years, Will Kellogg donated more than $66 million to his foundation, which took its direction from his belief that "education offers the greatest opportunity for really improving one generation over another." Kellogg encouraged his trustees to create new and innovative ways "to bring the greatest good to the greatest number." He continued to be involved in the activities of his foundation for the rest of his life, but he allowed his trustees to make decisions.

Though legally blind from glaucoma by the time he reached the age of 80, Kellogg remained active in the work of the foundation, attending meetings accompanied by one of his German shepherd dogs—all descendants of the film star Rin-Tin-Tin. (Although not trained as "Seeing Eye" dogs, as was often erroneously reported, they were faithful and helpful companions.) Kellogg lost his eyesight, but not his vision of a better future for others.

On October 6, 1951, W. K. Kellogg died at the age of 91. Since that time, the trustees of the W. K. Kellogg Foundation have continued the philosophy of its founder: "To help people help themselves through the practical application of knowledge and resources to improve their quality of life and that of future generations."

*Artist Norman Rockwell (1894-1978), who
specialized in painting warm and humorous scenes of
everyday people, created these appealing faces for the
Kellogg Company in the mid-1950s.*

From modest beginnings, with programs serving
the health and education needs of youth in south-central
Michigan, Kellogg's foundation has grown to achieve
national and international prominence. In 1996, the
W. K. Kellogg Foundation ranked second among foundations in both assets (more than $6 billion) and amount
of annual donations ($222 million). Currently, it serves
the needs of people in the United States, Africa, Latin
America, and the Caribbean.

The W. K. Kellogg Foundation directs its grants toward three broad areas of human concern: health, agriculture, and education. The foundation promotes the health of the community through public health programs, disease prevention, and primary care. For example, the foundation granted $6 million to the Hospital Research and Education Trust in Chicago to develop model hospitals.

To support rural development, the foundation works to protect water supplies and to provide communities with safe, nutritious food systems. The W. K. Kellogg Foundation also supports efforts to strengthen youth development and higher education programs. In 1994, it granted gifts ranging between $2 and $5 million each to Indiana University, the University of Michigan, Tuskegee University, and Western Michigan University. In addition, the foundation also funds philanthropic and volunteer groups, such as the Urban League, that are committed to solving community problems and to improving human life.

Always an independent organization, today the foundation is the Kellogg Company's largest stockholder, using over $100 million a year in dividends to help fund its programs. True to the wishes of its founder, Will Keith Kellogg, the foundation directs its resources toward changes that will improve the well-being of people by helping people to help themselves.

Catherine T. MacArthur (1906-1981) helped her husband John D. MacArthur (1897-1978) accumulate a fortune from insurance companies and real estate holdings. The foundation that bears their names is one of the largest in the world.

8

John D. and Catherine T. MacArthur
Let Others Decide

*J*ohn D. MacArthur liked to take risks, to find adventure, and to say and do outrageous things, sometimes just to shock those around him. Starting with nothing but his own drive for success, he was a millionaire at age 45.

Claiming that he had no idea how rich he was, MacArthur said, "Anyone who knows what he's worth isn't worth very much." But by other people's reckoning, this eccentric billionaire was the second richest man in the United States when he died in 1978. (Only shipping tycoon Daniel Ludwig was thought to be wealthier at the time.) And the amount of money MacArthur gave away at his death has made the foundation he created and named for himself and his wife, Catherine, one of the most richly endowed in the country today.

John Donald MacArthur was born on March 6, 1897, in Pittston, Pennsylvania. He was the youngest of seven children raised in a strict household dominated by his father, William, a well-known biblical preacher. John's mother, Georgiana, who suffered from her husband's harshness and indifference, was grateful when he was away on a preaching mission. William believed that to spare the rod was to spoil the child. So, when he was home, he often disciplined his boys by using a vinegar-soaked leather strap on their backs. In spite of this severe treatment, the boys were irrepressible, always thinking up some new and daring prank.

In 1910, the family moved to Nyack, New York, where John and his brother, Charles, attended the Wilson Academy. Relieved to be free of their father's repression, the two brothers became the most mischievous students at the school. In fact, John became better known for his boldness than for his studies.

John left school in the eighth grade and, after his mother died in 1915, he joined his older brothers in Chicago. Each of his three brothers had become successful in different fields of endeavor. Alfred, the oldest, was a prominent insurance executive. Telfer went to work for a chain of suburban newspapers and owned the chain

The MacArthur family. John is seated at the bottom, in the center.

by the time he was 25. Charles, the maverick to whom John felt closest, became a journalist and later a screenwriter. With Ben Hecht, he coauthored the Pulitzer Prize-winning play, *The Front Page*. Along the way, Charles also married actress Helen Hayes.

Settled in Chicago but needing a job, John worked as an office helper in Alfred's insurance company. When he became bored with his menial tasks, he went out to sell insurance and discovered he had a talent for sales. At age 19, he sold $1 million worth of insurance policies in one year.

In 1917, with his country's entry into World War I, John enlisted in the U.S. Navy. Dissatisfied with the navy, he deserted and went to Canada and joined the Royal Canadian Air Force. His tour of duty ended abruptly when he crashed his plane, badly injuring his back. He spent weeks in a hospital, where he became increasingly impatient with his long recovery.

Wanting to go back into action, MacArthur stowed away on a troop train bound for New York. Before reaching his destination, however, he was discovered and turned over to military authorities. Although MacArthur could have been severely punished, he had the good fortune to have become acquainted with a young journalist who wrote a sensational story about him. She called him a patriotic young man who was making an extreme effort to serve his country, even before his injuries were healed. Consequently, John MacArthur, the deserter, became John MacArthur, the hero.

In the face of such publicity, the U.S. Navy decided to give MacArthur a simple discharge that declared him "unfit for military service." The Royal Canadian Air Force, however, gave him an honorable discharge.

After the war, MacArthur returned to Chicago to again sell insurance in his brother's office. Meeting with some success, in 1919 he married Louise Ingalls, a socially prominent young woman with whom he had two children, Roderick and Virginia. Unfortunately, John and Louise were never interested in the same way of life. While she wanted a loving, quiet home life, John was only interested in business and worked long hours. The couple separated and eventually divorced.

Still working for Alfred, MacArthur now became interested in Catherine Hyland, his brother's secretary. They were a perfect match. Catherine, the daughter of Irish immigrants who had settled on Chicago's South Side, was an experienced businesswoman who shared John's ambition and understood his compulsive work habits. They were married in 1926.

In 1928, MacArthur found an opportunity to become independent of his brother. Through a friend, he learned of a small, financially troubled insurance company, Marquette Life, in Jerseyville, Illinois. He and Catherine bought the company for $7,500. By working together and using their managerial skills, experience, and drive to succeed, they managed to turn the company around in just over a year.

In 1929, just when MacArthur's success seemed assured, the stock market crashed, putting the entire nation into the Great Depression. In the ensuing panic, people cashed in their insurance policies for needed money, and sales came to a standstill. Companies larger than Marquette were going under, but with hard work, John and Catherine managed to keep their small company solvent.

John's determination was fed by his desire to show his brothers that he could be successful. "I had shot my mouth off to my brothers about making a big success," he later declared, "So I couldn't throw in the sponge when things got tough after '29."

In 1935, with Catherine's approval, John took another risk. He heard about a company being forced to go out of business because of a $2,500 debt. MacArthur borrowed the $2,500 needed to buy the poorly managed Bankers Life and Casualty. He brought home the company's records in a single box and set it on the kitchen table. Then he and Catherine went to work. This insurance company formed the foundation for what would become MacArthur's financial empire.

The MacArthurs worked long hours to keep their two companies alive through the worst of times. The two were a perfect team. An extrovert and a risk taker, John was a great salesman. Catherine's strength as a business administrator gave her the judgment to know when to hold John back if some of his ventures appeared too risky. Under her maiden name, Catherine appears in the records of John's various companies as corporate secretary, director, or both.

Despite their efforts, Bankers Life and Casualty struggled. Then John discovered a revolutionary idea. The former management had devised a plan that charged $1-per-month for a $1,000 policy, but they had never attempted to sell it. MacArthur immediately recognized the plan's potential. With Catherine's encouragement, he marketed the policy through direct-mail solicitations.

The response turned out to be greater than they had anticipated. Putting its initial profits into large-scale advertising, the company moved ahead. Between 1940 and 1950, MacArthur sold hundreds of thousands of these low-cost policies. Still compelled to show his brothers that he could succeed, MacArthur worked 14-hour days, six days a week, until, by 1958, Bankers Life had grown into a billion-dollar enterprise.

During this period, the MacArthurs bought other insurance companies, merging them with Bankers Life. These acquisitions brought both experienced sales-people and growing financial assets into the business. MacArthur began to build an empire, adding banks, utilities, radio and television stations, hotels, and apartment and office buildings in New York City.

When Florida was booming in the 1960s, he owned 100,000 acres of land there—more than any other individual. Real estate investments made up the largest part of MacArthur's millions, but it had been the profits from the insurance company that provided the money to purchase those holdings.

With all his millions, MacArthur never took on the manners or comforts of the newly rich. After moving from Chicago to Florida in 1958, he conducted his business from a rear table in the coffee shop of an aging resort, the Colonnades Beach Hotel, that he owned in

John MacArthur at work in his "office" in the Colonnades Beach Hotel coffee shop. An extrovert who loved talking to people, MacArthur would speak with anyone who walked in the coffee shop. Waitresses would usher visitors to and from his table.

Palm Beach Shores. Here he made himself available to anyone who sought him out. He and Catherine lived in the hotel in a simply furnished, two-bedroom apartment overlooking the parking lot.

MacArthur preferred a frugal way of life, wearing rumpled clothes and driving a dusty old car. With a keen sense of humor, MacArthur enjoyed being outrageous, often shocking people with his penny-pinching. He sometimes handed friends the check after inviting them for a meal or wrapped up half-finished sandwiches to take home.

To his great satisfaction, MacArthur's insurance empire of more than a dozen companies far exceeded his brother Alfred's large firm. He once told a reporter he was grateful to Alfred for two things: "For teaching me the principles of the insurance business and for telling me I couldn't make it on my own. I wouldn't have gotten anywhere if I hadn't had to show him how wrong he was."

MacArthur had a knack for gathering capable executives into his company. Often involved in lawsuits, he developed an expert legal department. His general counsel, William Kirby, also became his close confidant and friend.

MacArthur was not a charitable man during his lifetime. He claimed to be too busy making money to get involved in giving his money away. "If people knew an old guy was sitting here giving away money," he once said from his office, "this [place] would be full of people and I wouldn't be free to lead the kind of life I like." But when MacArthur reached the age of 70, Kirby advised him to set up a foundation to distribute his vast wealth upon his death. Kirby told MacArthur he had two choices. He could either allow a sizeable percentage of his fortune to go to the government in taxes, or he could set up a foundation. By doing the latter, a board of directors of his own choosing would decide how his money should be spent after his death.

Kirby had made his point. On October 19, 1970, the John D. and Catherine T. MacArthur Foundation came into being. Catherine's name, not originally included on the papers, was added at John's direction: "Change the name to include Catherine," he stipulated. "She helped make it, too."

After MacArthur carefully selected his foundation's board of trustees, he took no further interest in how his money would be distributed. Like George Eastman and Julius Rosenwald, John D. MacArthur did not believe in directing the disbursement of his money from his grave. He trusted his board to carry out the responsibility of disbursing the funds. "You guys will have to figure out after I am dead what to do with it," he bluntly told them.

John Donald MacArthur died from cancer of the pancreas eight years later on January 6, 1978, in West Palm Beach, Florida. Catherine continued to serve on the board of the foundation until her death, also from cancer, in 1981.

When the trustees first met following MacArthur's death, they had the advantage of complete freedom to develop a philanthropic program. But they lacked the benefit of any direction from the founder. The trustees ultimately decided to focus on a limited number of areas of human endeavor.

With the foundation funded with $700 million, World Resources, Inc., an environmental research center, was established. The foundation supported efforts to control diseases caused by parasites, such as malaria. (These diseases claim more victims worldwide than cancer.) Other initial programs focused on the fields of mental health; efforts for peace and international cooperation; cultural programs in the MacArthurs' two home communities, Chicago and Palm Beach; and grants to foster individual creativity—the MacArthur Fellows Program. The Fellows Program, dubbed the "genius grants," has stirred the public's interest and imagination. Believing in the potential of creative individuals to contribute to human progress, unrestricted grants of money are provided as fellowships.

These fellowships differ from most grant-making trusts in that individuals cannot apply or ask to be considered. Instead, the foundation solicits nominations from a group of more than 100 designated nominators, who are drawn from a wide range of professional and academic fields. During a given year, the nominators submit names to a small selection committee for review. The committee then gives their recommendations to the foundation's board of directors. The criteria that must be met before a name is submitted include potential for future work as reflected in past achievements, evidence of the recipient's financial need, and a belief that the work is significant and important to society.

These fellowships, which allow recipients to spend the money however they wish, differ in another important way. Few individual grants span more than a year or two. Recipients of MacArthur fellowships receive five-year stipends ranging from $30,000 to $75,000 annually. The length of the fellowships frees the winners to concentrate entirely on their work. Among the MacArthur prize winners have been Russian poet Joseph Brodsky, sociologist Sara Lawrence Lightfoot, paleontologist Stephen Jay Gould, and Harlem school teacher Deborah Meier.

Today, the Foundation seeks to respond to new needs, such as reducing inequities in society and solving world-population problems. "Sponsored by the John D. and Catherine T. MacArthur Foundation" is a familiar phrase to listeners of National Public Radio and viewers of public television stations. The foundation also continues its commitment to strengthening the MacArthurs' home communities of Chicago and Palm Beach through the arts, cultural programs, education, and community development. Each year, the foundation makes hundreds of grants to museums, musicians, and theater and dance

Writer and independent filmmaker John Sayles (right) received a MacArthur "genius grant" in 1983. Shown on the set with child actor David Strathairn, Sayles directed Eight Men Out, *a film about the 1919 World Series during which the Chicago White Sox accepted money to lose.*

companies to help as many diverse ethnic groups as possible.

Since its inception in 1970, the John D. and Catherine T. MacArthur Foundation has grown to more than $3 billion in assets. In the mid-1990s, it provided $2.9 million annually for grants, which, based on total giving, made it the fifth-largest philanthropic foundation in the United States.

*John D. Rockefeller donated more than $45 million
to the University of Chicago and called his gifts "the
best investment I ever made." Julius Rosenwald was
a trustee as well as a donor of over $6 million to the
university, shown above.*

148

The 25 Largest U.S. Foundations

(Based on gifts distributed by each foundation during the 1994 or 1995 fiscal year.)

Name	Total Gifts	Assets
1. The Ford Foundation	$285,226,002	$6,600,562,000
2. W. K. Kellogg Foundation	222,691,781	6,034,576,655
3. The Pew Charitable Trusts	157,169,536	3,298,723,548
4. The Robert Wood Johnson Foundation	135,861,955	3,754,153,612
5. John D. and Catherine T. MacArthur Foundation	116,279,275	2,914,554,520
6. The Annenberg Foundation	112,996,033	1,387,238,383
7. The Andrew W. Mellon Foundation	105,627,655	2,191,323,000
8. Lilly Endowment Inc.	99,354,052	3,093,752,921
9. The Rockefeller Foundation	93,260,988	2,364,552,922
10. Robert W. Woodruff Foundation, Inc.	63,217,640	1,732,729,896
11. The David and Lucile Packard Foundation	62,745,546	1,544,060,433
12. The Kresge Foundation	60,083,081	1,470,803,425
13. DeWitt Wallace-Reader's Digest Fund, Inc.	58,925,583	996,413,188
14. Soros Humanitarian Foundation	54,166,275	67,653,205
15. The McKnight Foundation	53,800,000	1,100,000,000
16. The Annie E. Casey Foundation	52,919,831	1,057,683,986
17. Charles Stewart Mott Foundation	51,505,688	1,203,825,430
18. The Harry and Jeannette Weinberg Foundation, Inc.	51,000,000	990,900,000
19. The New York Community Trust	50,965,342	964,123,681
20. The Duke Endowment	48,002,147	1,260,115,470
21. Carnegie Corporation of New York	45,723,708	1,126,710,522
22. The Starr Foundation	45,061,546	1,053,640,633
23. Arthur S. DeMoss Foundation	44,645,433	321,830,798
24. Lila Wallace-Reader's Digest Fund, Inc.	43,539,839	756,689,830
25. Alfred P. Sloan Foundation	40,986,123	789,637,993

149

Bibliography

Books:

Ackerman, Carl William. *George Eastman.* Boston: Houghton Mifflin, 1930.

Bowman, John S. *Andrew Carnegie.* Englewood Cliffs, N.J.: Silver Burdett, 1989.

Brayer, Elizabeth. *George Eastman: A Biography.* Baltimore: The Johns Hopkins University Press, 1996.

Carnegie, Andrew. *Autobiography of Andrew Carnegie.* Boston: Houghton Mifflin, 1920.

Coe, Brian. *George Eastman and the Early Photographers.* East Sussex, England: Wayland, 1988.

Coffey, Ellen Greenman. *John D. Rockefeller: Empire Builder.* Englewood Cliffs, N.J.: Silver Burdett, 1989.

Flint, John. *Cecil Rhodes.* Boston: Little, Brown, 1974.

The Foundation Directory. New York: The Foundation Center, 1995, 1996.

Gleasner, Diana C. *Dynamite.* New York: Walker, 1982.

Gray, Tony. *Champions of Peace: The Story of Alfred Nobel, the Peace Prize and the Laureates.* New York: Paddington Press, 1976.

Graymont, Barbara. *The MacArthur Heritage: The Story of an American Family.* Chicago: The John D. and Catherine T. MacArthur Foundation, 1993.

Halasz, Nicholas. *Nobel.* New York: Orion Press, 1959.

Hawke, David Freeman. *John D.: The Founding Father of the Rockefellers.* New York: Harper & Row, 1980.

Holbrook, Stewart H. *The Age of the Moguls.* Garden City, N.Y.: Doubleday, 1953.

Jarette, Alfred. *Julius Rosenwald: Son of a Jewish Immigrant.* Greenville, S.C.: Southeastern University Press, 1975.

John D. MacArthur: The Man and His Legacy. Chicago: The John D. and Catherine T. MacArthur Foundation, 1988.

Joseph, James A. *The Charitable Impulse.* New York: The Foundation Center, 1989.

Judson, Clara Ingram. *Andrew Carnegie.* Chicago: Follett, 1964.

Kanfer, Stefan. *The Last Empire.* New York: Farrar Straus Giroux, 1993.

McCarthy, Kathleen D. *Noblesse Oblige: Charity and Cultural Philanthropy in Chicago, 1849-1929.* Chicago: The University of Chicago Press, 1982.

Mitchell, Barbara. *Click! A Story about George Eastman.* Minneapolis: Carolrhoda, 1986.

Nielsen, Waldemar A. *The Golden Donors: A New Anatomy of the Great Foundations.* New York: Dutton, 1985.

Oldendahl, Theresa. *Charity Begins at Home.* New York: Basic Books, 1990.

Powell, Horace B. *The Original Has This Signature— W. K. Kellogg.* Battle Creek, Mich.: The Kellogg Foundation, 1956.

Rotberg, Robert I. *The Founder: Cecil Rhodes and the Pursuit of Power.* New York: Oxford University Press, 1988.

Werner, M. R. *Julius Rosenwald: The Life of a Practical Humanitarian.* New York: Harper & Row, 1939.

Annual Reports:

"Annual Report: A Portrait of Human Investment." Battle Creek, Mich.: W. K. Kellogg Foundation, 1994.

"Annual Report." New York: Carnegie Corporation of New York, 1994.

"Annual Report." New York: The Rockefeller Foundation, 1994.

"Report On Activities." Chicago: The John D. and Catherine T. MacArthur Foundation, 1993.

Index

154

159

ABOUT THE AUTHOR

CAROL G. TRAUB is the author of numerous magazine articles and stories for children and adults. She and her husband divide their time between Indiana and California, where they are involved in many philanthropic endeavors. They have three grown children and two young grandchildren.

Photo Credits

Photographs courtesy of: pp. 6, 147, Archive Photos; pp. 10, 48, 100, Bettmann Archives; pp. 14, 31 (all), 50, 58, 61, 62, 64, 66, 73, 75, 78, 79, 84, 85, 86, 98, 148, Library of Congress; pp. 19, 21, 24, 25, 27, 29, The Nobel Foundation; pp. 32, 37, 38, 40, 43, National Archives of Zimbabwe; pp. back cover (middle), 52, 59, Carnegie Corporation of New York; 70, 81, 83, Rockefeller Archive Center; pp. 90, 92, 94, 101, Sears, Roebuck, and Co.; pp. 102, 105, 107, 111, 113, 116, George Eastman House; pp. 127, 132, Kellogg Company; pp. 118, 121, 123, 129, W. K. Kellogg Foundation; pp. 134, 137, 142, John D. and Catherine T. MacArthur Foundation.